Date Due

THE AMERICAN WAY WEST

Adapted from TO THE ENDS OF THE EARTH
by Irene M. Franck and David M. Brownstone

A Volume in the Trade and Travel Routes Series

Facts On File
New York • Oxford

THE AMERICAN WAY WEST

Facts On File, Inc.   Facts On File Limited
460 Park Avenue South   Collins Street
New York NY 10016   Oxford OX4 1XJ
USA   United Kingdom

Library of Congress Cataloging-in-Publication Data

The American way west: adapted from To the ends of the earth by Irene
M. Franck and David M. Brownstone.
       p. cm. — (Trade and travel routes)
    Includes bibliographical references and index.
    Summary: Traces the history of the following trade and travel routes: the
Mohawk Trail, the Wilderness Road and other trans-Appalachian routes, the
Mississippi Route, and the Santa Fe, Chihuahua, Oregon, and California
Trails.
    ISBN 0-8160-1880-4
    1. United States—Territorial expansion—Juvenile literature.   2. Frontier
and pioneer life—United States—Juvenile literature.   Trails—United
States—History—Juvenile literature. 4. Trade routes—United States—History—Juvenile literature. [1. United States—Territorial expansion.
2. Frontier and pioneer life. 3. Trails—History. 4. Trade routes—History.]
I. Franck, Irene M. To the ends of the earth. II. Brownstone, David M.
III. Series: Trade and travel routes series.
E179.5.A474 1990
973—dc20   90-37825

A British CIP catalogue record for this book is available from the British
Library.

Facts On File books are available at special discounts when purchased in
bulk quantities for businesses, associations, institutions, or sales promotions.
Please call our Special Sales Department in New York at 212/683-2244 (dial
800/322- 8755 except in NY, AK, or HI) or in Oxford at 865/728399.

Jacket design by Catherine Hyman
Composition by Facts On File, Inc.
Manufactured by R.R. Donnelley & Sons
Printed in the United States of America

10 9 8 7 6 5 4 3 2 1

This book is printed on acid-free paper.

CONTENTS

LIST OF MAPS

PREFACE

The American Way West is one volume in the Travel and Trade Routes series. The series is based on our earlier work, *To the Ends of the Earth*, published by Facts On File in 1984. This adaptation of the work for young readers has been prepared by Facts On File; many new illustrations have been added. The maps, drawn from *To the Ends of the Earth*, are by Dale Adams.

Irene M. Franck
David M. Brownstone
Chappaqua, New York

INTRODUCTION

WHAT IS A TRADE ROUTE?

In a world without airplanes, engine-powered ships, trucks, or even paved roads, how did people journey from one place to another? How did products that were found only in a very small part of the world eventually find their way to other parts of the world? For almost 5,000 years, people have been trading products from one part of the world to another using trade routes. Traders from Europe, Asia, and Africa carried furs, spices, silks, pottery, knives, stone utensils, jewels, and a whole host of other commodities, exchanging the products found in one area for the products found in another.

When trading first began, there were no real roads. Local traders might follow trails or cross steep mountain passes in their treks from one village to another. With the passage of time, tracks might be widened and eventually paved. But the new paved roads tended to follow the old trade routes, establishing these routes as important links of communication between different cultures.

As technology advanced, sea-lanes became vital trade routes between the various continents and made possible trade with North America, South America, and Australia. Many of the highways and seaways that have been used predominantly for trade throughout history have shaped the course of history because of the many ways in which the routes have been used.

WHY STUDY TRADE ROUTES?

Studying the trade routes of the world is one way of learning about the history of the world. As we look at the trade routes of Europe, for example, we can see how the nations of that continent have changed throughout the centuries: we learn how Scandinavian Vikings came to sail south and west to settle in France and Britain; we can appreciate how present-day Hungary was originally settled by a wandering tribe from the Ural Mountains, etc. In a similar way, by looking at the trade routes of Africa, we can trace the history of the slave trade, and learn about the European colonization of Africa in the 18th and 19th centuries.

In addition, studying the trade routes helps us better understand the origin of many of the institutions and services with which we are familiar today. Postal systems, tolls, guidebooks, roadside restaurants, and hotels have all come into being, either directly or indirectly, because of trade routes. Studying the trade routes helps us to understand how they emerged.

How to Use This Book

This book is organized in chapters. Each chapter is devoted to the history of one trade route or, in some cases, where the particular trade route has a particularly long and eventful history, to a particular era in a trade route's history. Therefore, you can simply read about one trade route that particularly interests you or, alternatively, read about all the trade routes in a given area. At the end of each chapter, you will find a list of books for further reading, which will assist you in locating other resources should you need them to support report research or classroom work. If you are using this book as a reference book for a particular history course, check the index to find the information on the subject or person of interest to you. The list of maps at the front of this book will direct you to all maps contained in this book, and thereby help you to locate each trade route.

Studying trade routes can be a fascinating way of learning about world history—and of understanding more about our lives today. We hope you enjoy all the volumes in the Trade and Travel Routes series.

1

THE MOHAWK TRAIL

PATHWAY TO THE WEST

The great human pathway called the Mohawk Trail was a major passage to the heartland of North America. It began as a footpath through a natural separation between the Catskill and Adirondack Mountains, part of the long Appalachian range, in New York State. The Appalachian range, extending from mid-Georgia to Canada, divides the east coast of North America from the rest of the continent. It is cut by only one easy, level land route to the western lands. This is the valley of the Mohawk River, called "Te-non-an-at-che," or "the river flowing through mountains," by early Native Americans. Thus, the Mohawk River Valley provided a natural passage linking New England and the Hudson River Valley with the Great Lakes and the Western Plains.

In its early history, the Mohawk Trail was used as the main route by Native Americans who were pushing east. Later, it became the route of colonists pushing west to settle the continent—and to send back the riches of the Midwest. Throughout its history, the Mohawk Trail has been not only a major migration route but also an economic lifeline and a spur for the development of New York City into a world capital. Because of its importance to so many groups of people, the trail also often has been a battleground, for at one time, control of the Mohawk Trail meant control of northeastern North America.

THE TRAIL

The original Mohawk Trail, also called the Iroquois Trail, ran along the well-drained banks on both sides of the Mohawk River Valley,

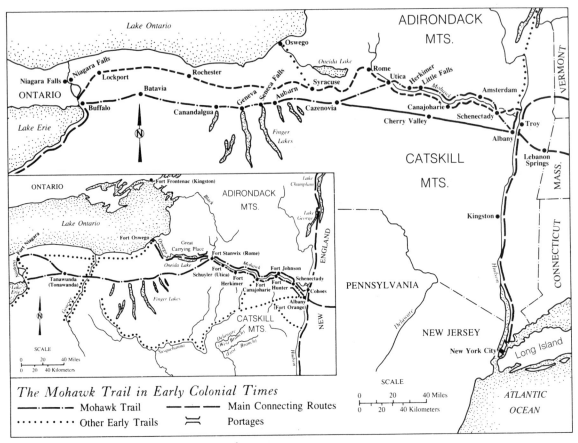

The Mohawk Trail in Early Colonial Times

——·—— Mohawk Trail   —— —— Main Connecting Routes

·········· Other Early Trails   ≍ Portages

The Mohawk Trail in the Early 1800s

——·—— Mohawk Trail

———— Great Western Turnpike

-------- Erie Canal

········ Main Connecting Canals

—— —— Main Connecting Roads

from Albany to Rome, New York. It then headed directly westward along the Ontario Plain, touching the tops of the Finger Lakes. Beyond the lakes, it passed through Tanawunda. This was the "great hearing place," near modern Batavia, where the distant Niagara Falls could be heard in the wilderness quiet. The trail reached the eastern end of Lake Erie, and there the whole heart of the continent opened out.

The Mohawk Trail was originally a footpath, probably following game trails for much of its route. It was beaten down by the Algonquin Indians who moved into northeastern North America

3,000–5,000 years ago, or perhaps even earlier. Tramped down several inches below normal ground level, the trail was narrow—only a foot or so wide, just enough so that walkers could proceed in single file. It was also winding, for the Indians made detours around natural obstacles such as rocks or fallen trees, rather than remove them. It was generally dark, dank, and muddy as well, for most of its route was through a dense forest of mature hardwoods and pines. When the trees were in leaf, they formed a canopy shutting out almost all light and warmth from above.

However poor and narrow, this network of trails formed the basic travel and trade routes for Native Americans in the northeast. The Mohawk Trail formed the main link between many other major land routes. Among these were the north-south Genesee Valley trails and the Catskill Trail, which ran southeast from the Genesee River to the Susquehanna near Binghamton and then northeast back up to Canajoharie and Albany. The Mohawk Trail also met the north-south Hudson River and Champlain Valley trails and the trails east from Albany and west through the Great Lakes.

The Mohawk River. The Mohawk Trail also linked with other major water routes. Early native Americans and later colonists often preferred to travel by water where they could. They portaged—that is, carried or dragged their canoes—around rapids and waterfalls or from one body of water to another. The Mohawk River itself was used as such a water route. Travelers from Lake Ontario moved up the Oswego River to Oneida Lake. Then they went up the small Wood Creek to the Great Carrying Place and portaged their

With the Mohawk River in the background, this Mohawk village has cabins and tents but no longhouses in view inside its wooden palisade. (Courtesy New York Public Library)

boats to the Mohawk River near Rome, New York. From there they were able to travel down the Mohawk, with some short portages, as far as Cohoes Falls. Landing at Schenectady, water travelers then joined the land trail on the 16-mile portage to Albany on the Hudson River.

THE NATIVE AMERICANS

In the early 17th century, the Native American people known as the Iroquois took control of the Mohawk Trail. For 400 years, the Iroquois had been moving east from the Mississippi Valley. By the early 1600s, they had pushed their rivals, the Algonquin Indians, east and south of Albany. Then commanding the trail, the Iroquois collected tribute or payment from surrounding tribes. Unlike the Algonquins, who were only loosely united, the Iroquois were a strong, tightly knit group of peoples. They were known as the "Brotherhood of Five Nations" or the "Brotherhood of the Long House," so-called after the long buildings in their towns and villages.

The easternmost of the Iroquois tribes were the Mohawks. They were called the "keepers of the eastern door of the long house," because of their position on the trail. Their enemies named them "Mohawks," meaning "eaters of living creatures." The name was meant to describe their strength when at war, but some early Europeans took it to be a charge of cannibalism. The other Iroquois tribes were—heading west along the Mohawk Trail—the Oneidas, the Onondagas, the Cayugas, and the Senecas. Later they were joined by a sixth tribe, the Tuscaroras. By the mid-17th century, the Iroquois had firm control of the Mohawk Trail. They had set up a network of runners along the main route and its connecting trails, providing steady, fast communication among the Iroquois nations.

THE EUROPEANS

French explorers, fur traders, and missionaries were the first Europeans to enter the region of the Mohawk Trail. In the early 1600s, they moved from the St. Lawrence River Valley and the Great Lakes to the Niagara River, which runs between Lake Ontario and Lake Erie. They took the Oswego River route to the Mohawk River.

Not long behind the French were the Dutch. They began fur trading along the eastern end of the Mohawk Trail in 1614. In 1624, the Dutch founded Fort Orange (now Albany) just south of the junction of the Hudson and Mohawk rivers. From there, the Dutch West India Company carried on an active trade with the Iroquois. They traded cloth, sewan and wampum (beads used for decoration and trade), axes, kettles, and other iron goods for fur skins to be shipped down the Hudson through the port of New Amsterdam (now New York) to Europe.

First Written Records of the Mohawk Trail. The Dutch were concerned about French fur trading on the eastern half of the trail. In 1634, the West India Company sent a party of three Dutchmen and five Mohawk guides to reach a trade agreement with the Iroquois. Herman Meyndertz van dan Bogaert, who was the company surgeon and leader of the party, provided the first written record of a trip along the Mohawk Trail. Traveling on foot and carrying backpacks, the party followed the trail from Fort Orange (Albany) northwest to the Mohawk River and then along the south bank of the river. The mid-December trip was especially hard, Bogaert said, "because it snowed very often up to the height of a man." Snow and rain also flooded the streams they had to cross. That made the trip doubly hard, as Bogaert described:

> This stream ran very fast; besides, big cakes of ice came drifting along, for the heavy rainfall...had set the ice drifting. We were in great danger, for if one of us had lost his footing it had cost us our lives; but God the Lord preserved us, and we came through safely....

Usually, there were no problems in securing lodgings. Iroquois villages dotted the route and welcomed the travelers. In one village, they stayed with the chief, who personally cooked their meal of beans and maize and took them to hunt turkeys when they could not go on "because all the footpaths had disappeared under the heavy snowfalls."

The party did not always reach such lodgings, however. At one point, Bogaert wrote, the road became so hard "that some of the savages had to stop in the forest and sleep in the snow. We went on, however, and reached a little cabin, where we slept." Like the cabin, not all the villages were inhabited.

In January 1635, the party finally arrived at the Oneida village, which lay along the portage route between Oneida Lake and the Mohawk River. When they reached the village, their welcome was not all they might have hoped for, for the French had caused the Oneidas to expect gifts:

...one of the council came to me, asking the reason for our coming into his land, and what we brought for him as a present. I told him that we did not bring any present, but that we only paid him a visit. He told us we were not worth anything, because we did not bring him a present.

The same council member was not satisfied with the prices offered by the Dutch traders. He called them "scoundrels" because they did not pay enough for their beaver skins. However, the Dutch finally got what they came for. The eastern Iroquois—the Mohawks and the Oneidas—agreed to trade only with the Dutch. The French, however, kept sole fur-trading rights on the western half of the trail.

Trading Wars. A series of trading wars began that affected the history of the Mohawk Trail for the next 150 years. The Iroquois found that the Dutch were better trading partners than the French. To get more goods to trade, the Iroquois took more tribute—in the form of furs—from the weaker tribes around them. At the same time, the French, Dutch, and English all battled for control of the area. In 1664, the English took over the Dutch territory and trading rights. They renamed Fort Orange as Albany and New Amsterdam as New York.

Problems in the area grew when the Europeans began to supply their valuable Iroquois allies with guns. The French had North American allies, too, especially the "praying Indians" they had converted to Catholicism. However, during the British-French struggle for control of the region, some French traders and missionaries lost their lives in Iroquois territory. But the French and their allies also caused damage. In 1690, they attacked almost the whole of the eastern end of the Mohawk Trail, burning Schenectady.

Peace Is Established. The following decades saw both war and uneasy peace. Most of the Mohawk Trail stayed in Iroquois control and the English continued their trade alliance with the Iroquois. This trade alliance was also to become a military alliance. English settlement was limited to the eastern portion of the trail, which left the western two-thirds of the trail to the Brotherhood of the Long House.

The Travels of John Bartram. Few outsiders passed through this western territory in the early 18th century. One who did, Philadelphia naturalist John Bartram, noted in 1743 that the route was "fine level rich land most of the way and tall timber oak, birch, beech, ash, spruce, linden, elm...and maidenhair in abundance." Oswego he called "an infant settlement," where the whole navigation in the region was "carried on by the Indians themselves in bark canoes." Strangers were treated with suspicion. Swedish botanist Peter Kahn experienced this treatment when he went to view the "Great Falls at Niagara." As he wrote to Bartram in 1750:

> ...The French there [at Fort Niagara] seemed much perplexed at my first coming, imagining I was an English officer who, under pretext of seeing Niagara Falls, came with some other view; but as soon as I shew'd them my passports they chang'd their behavior and received me with the greatest civility.

THE SETTLERS

On the eastern part of the trail—the Mohawk Valley itself—European settlement began to change the face of the land. Scotch-Irish, Palatine German, Dutch, and English farmers came. They were not content to be tenant farmers, working the acres of wealthy landowners and turning over part of their crops as rent. Instead, they started clearing and working small farms along the Mohawk River and its main feeder stream, the Schoharie. The Mohawk Trail, once tamped (packed down) only by moccasined feet, became firmer and wider under the passage of heavy hobnailed boots and the hooves of cattle and horses. Gradually, this part of the trail was widened to handle more traffic. For the first time, wheels began to cut ruts into the dirt path, as the farmers added food to the mix of goods traded along the trail.

The English Control the Route. Even in the fertile Mohawk Valley, settlement was sparse. This was the main battleground between the English and French for control of the Mohawk Trail and of North America. By the last of these wars, the French and Indian War (1754–63), the English held the western end of the Mohawk Trail, all the way to Fort Niagara. They had ended French trading south of the St. Lawrence Valley and the Great Lakes. The treaty ending the wars left the western part of the Mohawk Trail in Iroquois hands. Indeed, the British "proclamation line of 1763" forbade settlement west of Fort Stanwix (now Rome), at the beginning of the "Great Carrying Place" to Oneida Lake. In effect, the

Mohawk Trail had come under English control, and with it the key to the continent.

Maintaining the Trail. By 1763, when the fighting ended, a thin line of European settlements extended to Fort Stanwix, and the Mohawk Trail had become known as the "King Highway." Property owners were responsible for maintaining the roads in their local areas. Even members of the ruling class, such as Sir William Johnson, baronet of the Mohawk region, was responsible for performing 10 days' maintenance work on the road per year. Much of the work was clearing away each year's growth of underbrush. Trees had to be cut back from the sides, to widen the road. Swampy sections had to be "corduroyed." Corduroying meant placing 10- to 12-foot logs close together to provide a firmer, though often slippery, footing for people and animals. Large trees and other natural obstacles were usually left in place. Few bridges were built, although poles might be thrown across a stream, or steep banks near fording places might be cut through and graded, or made level, for easier crossing.

During the few years of peace, towns also began to develop, generally on the north side of the Mohawk River. By the 1770s, some eastern parts of the Mohawk Trail were made wide and straight enough for horse races to be held. But in the wilderness west of the European settlements, there were still only narrow footpaths. So stood the Mohawk Trail at the time of the American Revolution.

THE AMERICAN REVOLUTION

The Mohawk Valley was a dangerous place to live during the years of the revolutionary war. The settlers who supported the Revolution were exposed on the northwestern frontier. In the early years, they were far from any hope of support from their army. Because their crops helped feed that army, the area was called the "breadbasket to the Revolution." Aside from that, their main role was to keep the British forces and their allies—the Mohawks, Onondagas, Cayugas, and Senecas—from moving east along the Mohawk Trail. They did stop the British and Iroquois, in August of 1777, in the Battle of Oriskany, 10 miles east of Fort Stanwix.

The British Master Plan. In 1777, the British Army developed a master plan for defeating the rebels in North America. They envisioned a three-pronged attack on the Americans. One army would strike south from Montreal through the Champlain Valley. Another would march north from New York City through the Hudson Valley. The third would come east from Lake Ontario, along the Oswego River and past Oneida Lake, along the Mohawk Trail. The three armies were to converge on Albany, in upstate New York, splitting the Revolutionary forces and—perhaps more important —putting strong British forces at their rear.

The Battle of Oriskany. At Fort Stanwix (now Rome) near the northward curve of the Mohawk River, the ragtag rebels held off what they called "a banditti of robbers, murderers, and traitors, composed of savages of America, and more savage Britons." Even so, the cost of the Battle of Oriskany (near Stanwix) was very great. The rebel forces might not have withstood another attack, but their commander-in-chief, Benedict Arnold, fooled the British. He sent an Iroquois-raised boy named Hon Yost Schuyler into the British camp. Schuyler delivered a letter stating that Arnold's forces numbered 15,000. The British and their Iroquois allies then quickly retreated, and the British master plan collapsed.

The War Finally Ends. Although the British plan failed, the idea had been sound. The British knew the importance of controlling the Mohawk Trail and the crossroads at Albany. They had learned from the example of the Iroquois, French, and Dutch before them.

After Oriskany, the main battles were elsewhere in the colonies, but there were heavy Iroquois and British attacks all along the frontier. These kept up even after the defeat of the British under

By the 1790s a wide road extended on the north side of the Mohawk River, and much of the fertile valley land was under cultivation. (From *New York Magazine,* March 1793)

Burgoyne later in 1777 at Saratoga, north of the junction of the Mohawk and Hudson rivers. The Iroquois attacks became so strong that in 1779 George Washington sent troops against the Iroquois along the Mohawk Trail. This protected both the people of the frontier and the army's vital food supplies. The American troops fought their way deep into Iroquois territory. By the time the war ended, they had broken Iroquois power. Many Iroquois followed their British allies north into Canada after their defeat. The rest were powerless against the new Americans, who had gained control of the Mohawk Trail.

OPENING THE WEST

Settlement of the Land Around the Trail. After the revolutionary war, the whole western part of New York, centered on the Mohawk Trail, was opened to settlement. The remaining Iroquois were forced out and pushed into small reservations. The new government held 18 million acres of land taken from the Iroquois. Out of this, a military tract of over 1.5 million acres was set aside in the Finger Lakes area for war veterans, who had been promised free land for their services. Some families moved into the area immediately, not waiting for the legal right to do so. Many more waited until 1790, when the townships were laid out and named. At that time, lots were awarded to veterans or to those who had bought veterans' rights.

After settlement of a dispute between New York and Massachusetts over ownership, the rest of the land westward from the Finger Lakes to Lake Erie was also opened up for settlement. Much of the land was bought by investment companies, including the Holland Land Company, which bought up the fertile Genesee Valley. In 1787, one New England veteran, Eliphalet Stark, moved to the Oneida Woods on the frontier near Fort Stanwix. He described the western New York wilderness at the time:

> ...it seemed like walking forever through an empty dark world of trees where the sun stopped in the upper branches, where the lakes were cold as Nantuckett water and as big as a Massachusetts county.

He noted that "if they ever got roads beyond the frontier at the carrying place at Fort Stanwix all of New England would be over to settle." How right he was.

The result of opening the Mohawk Trail was a migration the likes of which had never been seen by the young country. People came from the Hudson Valley, from New Jersey, Pennsylvania, and Maryland, and most of all from New England.

The New England Paths

The migration of people from New England was so great that the name "Mohawk Trail" was extended to cover several of the routes that led from the Atlantic to Albany. Like the original Mohawk Trail, these routes were old Native American trails, now used and developed by the new Americans. Emigrants from Massachusetts took the Old Bay Path from Boston west through Worcester to Springfield. There they were joined by southern New Englanders who took the Connecticut Path, which ran up the Connecticut River Valley. Together they crossed the Berkshire Hills going northwest through Lebanon Springs to join the old Mohawk Trail at Albany. Others from northern New England crossed from southern Vermont, on what is now U.S. Route 2, to the Hudson Valley at Troy.

The Boston Post Roads. The Boston-to-Springfield part of the Old Bay Path was also the route of the Old Boston Post Road. Post roads were roads made for carrying mail. The Old Boston Post Road went on to New Haven, where it joined another leg of the Post Road, which ran from Boston along the Atlantic shore. The two Boston Post roads joined at New Haven and continued to New York City. From there, the main post roads ran south to Philadelphia and all the way to Charleston, South Carolina.

In the years before the Revolution, these post roads had linked the British colonies along the Atlantic coast. Even after the Revolution, when the push was mostly westward, this string of post roads remained a vital line connecting the new states and grew with the young country. Later, much of this route was honored with the title of U.S. Route 1, running from Maine all the way south to Florida along the coast.

Between 1790 and 1800, over 60,000 people moved along all these New England paths and journeyed along the Mohawk Trail to settle the lands west all the way from Rome to Buffalo. By 1810, nearly 200,000 had moved to the west. On a single February day in 1795, one observer counted over 500 sleighs passing through Albany on their way west.

Eliphalet Stark, who foresaw the migration of New Englanders to the frontier, underestimated the time it would take before the great numbers of people pushed their way west. He thought "...it will be a hundred years before they ever got roads to the [Great] Lakes through these forests." He thought too little of his contemporaries. In the 50 years after Stark arrived along the Mohawk, almost 1 million people had moved into the western New York lands, building roads as they went. With the Mohawk Trail open, many other pioneers pushed straight on past New York State. They moved west along the strip of plain on the southern rim of Lake Erie and then into the Great Plains of the Midwest. In the early days of this great migration, many people preferred to travel in winter. A frozen path, or even a frozen river surface, was much easier than a muddy trail. Farmers, who did not have as much work in the winter anyway, would arrive in time for spring planting, sometimes sending for the other family members only then. But the urge to move west was soon too strong to be bound by the seasons.

The Demand for Good Roads. With the growth of long-distance traffic along the Mohawk Trail, passable roads became a public and business need. Not only were people traveling west, but also a rising volume of freight was being shipped back east and down the Hudson River. Local citizens could not maintain roads fit to handle such volume. New Yorkers turned to other methods of building and

Many of the early turnpikes were straight cuts, carved out of the mature forests, like this one with farmland beside it. (From Weld's *Travels Through the States of North America...1795, 1796, and 1797*, London, 1800)

maintaining roads. From 1790 on, the state directly paid those who built roads or bridges on what was then still state land. Lotteries were also used to raise money for road building. In 1797, lottery money was used to build the Great Genesee Road. This was a log-and-gravel road, 64 feet wide, running along the route of the old Mohawk Trail for 100 miles from Utica west to Geneva.

Toll Roads. Most long-distance road building in this period was carried on by the turnpike method, in which stock companies financed the building of wider, firmer roads. Maintenance—and company profits, if any—came from tolls paid by travelers using the route. Tollgates blocked the road, usually every 10 miles, and were opened to allow travelers through after payment of a toll.

Turnpikes on the Mohawk Trail. The first turnpike along the Mohawk Trail was built in 1797 between Schenectady and Albany. This important 16-mile stretch of road carried freight from both the land and water routes, following the path of the old portage between the Mohawk and the Hudson rivers. It was completed in 1805, and soon other turnpikes were built.

The Mohawk Turnpike ran from Schenectady to Utica, and the Rensselaer and Columbia Turnpike from Albany to Springfield, Massachusetts. The Great Genesee Road was converted to a turnpike and then extended farther west. After the War of 1812, it went all the way to Lake Erie. These turnpikes were so heavily used that a shortcut was made. It ran west from Albany south of the Mohawk River, through Cherry Valley and Cazenovia, and linked up with the main turnpike south of Oneida Lake.

In most cases, these highways followed the line of the old trails, but if the surveyors and engineers could remove a natural obstacle or cut a shorter, straighter route, they did so. To meet the needs of wheeled traffic, profitable toll ferries worked at key water crossings. Wooden bridges, some of them covered, were built.

LIFE ON THE ROAD

With the turnpike system in place, the Mohawk Trail was fully opened up. Hundreds of thousands of emigrants traveled over these roads. Many were from the New England states, but many others were fresh from Europe, traveling from the port of New York City up the Hudson River and then on the easiest route to the west—the Mohawk Trail.

The Stagecoach Arrives. Regular stagecoach lines were established to use the turnpikes. The first weekly stage along the Mohawk Trail began in 1793 over the 16-mile stretch of road between Albany and Schenectady. As soon as the Great Genessee Road opened, a stagecoach line was set up to run along it. The stagecoaches carried passengers from Utica to the new Geneva Hotel in just three days. These stagecoaches also transported mail, newspapers, and other important items such as banknotes and business documents to the townspeople along the way.

Wagoners along the Route. Sharing the road with stagecoaches, emigrant wagons, and local farm carts, were teamsters and drovers. They took goods and livestock along the line, usually eastward for shipment down the Hudson River. The teamsters, also called wagoners, drove large canvas-covered wagons pulled by teams of four to eight horses. A wagoner would sometimes ride a horse near the wagon wheel, but more often would walk alongside the team, holding a line to the lead horse and guiding the team with a whip. While doing this, wagoners wore footpaths by the side of the turnpike. Drovers, too, operated along the turnpikes. They bought animals along the route going east, put together herds of cattle or hogs or even flocks of turkeys, and sold them at markets near the Hudson River.

To provide food and shelter for all these travelers, taverns called "ordinaries" were set up all along the line. In some places, such as near the crossroads at Albany, there were as many as one tavern per mile. Each tavern usually catered to a particular group of travelers. Wagoners and drovers had their own taverns, as did the other travelers, such as those who could afford to charter a private coach. Many poorer emigrants simply camped alongside the road. Wagoners and drovers often carried oilcloths, which provided rough cover for themselves and their horses. They used these when taverns were overcrowded.

A Network of Towns and Roads. Traffic and population grew very rapidly. Along the main routes, towns seemed to spring up overnight. As settlers spread out in all directions, feeder roads and turnpikes were quickly built. Drovers often preferred these less-traveled, softer-surfaced roads, since the harder-surfaced turnpikes tended to lame their animals. The turnpikes were used more and more by heavily loaded wagons, which damaged the road by cutting them with their narrow wheels. Some turnpike companies even offered toll-free passage to wagons with wide wheels, which would pack down rather than carve up the roads. When turnpikes were in very bad condition, government inspectors forced turnpike companies to suspend collection of tolls until the roads were repaired. As the population grew in western New York, the flow of people and supplies west was equaled by the flow of goods back east; grain, fruit, animals, lumber, and other products flowed along the Mohawk Trail and down the Hudson River to New York City.

Waterways West

The water routes along the Mohawk Trail were also being improved. Through the revolutionary war period, the largest boats that were used on the Mohawk River were *bateaux*. These were flat-bottomed barge-like boats, poled or pulled from towpaths by 8–10 men. Each bateau could carry one to two tons of freight. These loaded bateaux had to be pulled like sledges along the shore, across portages, and around falls and rapids in the river. In 1797, Eliphalet Stark reported that his wife and baby and furniture traveled from Albany to Old Fort Schuyler (Utica) in 10 days, and that "it took six yokes of oxen to get their bateau around the carry at Little Falls." He also speculated about the future of the region:

> ...if they ever get a canal around Little Falls and one across the carrying place at Fort Stanwix, these Mohawk Dutch will begin to see things happen along the river that will make their eyes pop.

Stark proved to be right. Starting in the early 1790s, short stretches of canal were built to go around some difficult areas. By 1796, the Mohawk water route was open to flat-bottomed Durham boats all the way from Schenectady to Seneca Falls. These could carry 15–16 tons of goods and were large enough to have decks and sails.

New Land Routes Are Sought. Although the Durham boats cut the costs of shipping along the river, overland shipping costs for the farmers of western New York were still high. These farmers, and those of Ohio and the Midwest, began to try other routes for their crops. Some sent them down the Mississippi River to New Orleans or up the Great Lakes–St. Lawrence Route to Montreal. Others sent their crops by land, on turnpikes through the Appalachian Mountains to other ports, such as Baltimore or Pittsburgh.

THE ERIE CANAL–HUDSON RIVER ROUTE

In 1810, New Yorkers decided they would build an inland water route through the Mohawk River Valley, connecting the Great Lakes with the Hudson and the Atlantic. The Hudson had long been one of the great rivers of eastern North America. The Hudson and Mohawk valleys together were the best way through the Appalachian Mountains and out into the heartland of North America. A water route all the way from the great harbor of New York City to the flat, open lands of the Midwest would speed up communication and transportation considerably. This single move— the building of the Erie Canal—eventually made New York City the greatest port in the country and one of the world's greatest cities.

The canal had been proposed as early as 1783, by Irish-American engineer Christopher Colles. It became a reality, mainly through the efforts of a group led by DeWitt Clinton, who later became Governor of New York State. Getting the plan for the canal approved was not easy. Many sharply opposed it, calling it "Clinton's Ditch."

New Yorkers had good reason for celebrating the opening of the Erie Canal, for it would make their city a world metropolis. (Museum of the City of New York)

The Route of the Canal. The first Erie Canal ran side by side with the Mohawk River for part of its course and rose the 564 feet from Albany to Buffalo. The eastern section ran mostly on the south side of the Mohawk River (it was later rerouted to the north side). The western section was built somewhat north of the original Mohawk Trail. It passed through—and made the fortunes of—cities such as Syracuse and Rochester.

Construction of the Erie Canal was begun in 1817. It was completed in 1825 with the ceremonial "Marriage of the Waters," when DeWitt Clinton poured a bucket of Lake Erie water into the Atlantic Ocean off New York City.

Passengers and traders immediately started using the Erie Canal, and the new turnpike system almost went bankrupt. The cost of shipping grain from Buffalo to Albany had dropped from $100 a ton to $6. As a result, almost all crops from the upper Mississippi and Ohio valleys were funneled through the Erie Canal to New York City, which then supplied the whole of the East Coast and Europe.

Traffic on the Canal. On the new canal, the old bateaux and Durham boats were quickly superseded. Now there were heavy freight boats and passenger packets that carried 30 tons and, after 1830, up to 75 tons. Along with the freight came a flood of new immigrants from all over northern Europe. Among them were many Irish workers who helped to build the canal and stayed to settle along its route. The new canal inspired stories and folk songs that

This canal boat is riding high in the water at a lock; when the water is let out, the boat will drop to the lower level and pass under the bridge, with a cry for all rooftop passengers of "Low bridge, everybody down!" so they did not bump their heads. (New York Public Library, *View on the Erie Canal, 1830-1832,* watercolor drawing by J. W. Hill)

described travel conditions. The line "Low bridge, everybody down," from the song " The Erie Canal," was actually the warning given to passengers who rode on the cabin roofs on sunny days. The "mule named Sal" mentioned in the song is a reference to the animals that pulled the boats along the towpaths beside the canal.

Emigrants of the time were packed in crowded boats—"like two mice in a mitten," as one traveler of the time described it. But all the way to the "far West" of Illinois, Indiana, Wisconsin, Minnesota, and Michigan they sang of the people who "dug a mighty ditch" to let them "…sail upon the waters to Mich-i-gan-i-ay…"

With the steady flow of immigrants, and the plentiful supply of raw materials and water power, industry also began to build up along the Erie Canal. The coming of the steamboat also greatly helped foster trade and industry along the canal. Although the turnpike system had suffered when the canal first opened, it did not collapse. There was soon enough traffic for both. Indeed, the Erie Canal became crowded with slow freight. Most passengers, except for the long-distance emigrants needing cheap passage, took the faster stagecoach lines, which also continued to carry the mail.

More important, the Erie Canal was closed by ice four to five months a year. By contrast, in winter the stagecoach lines set speed records, sometimes over frozen roads, but more often along the hard ice surface of the Mohawk River and the Erie Canal. Some lines even moved their routes north for the season, and sped along the frozen southern edge of Lake Ontario. But soon both road and canal had a new rival: the railroad.

Early trains along the Mohawk Trail were simply a group of stagecoaches linked together, running on wooden tracks. (New York Central System)

In 1831, the first railroad was built along the Mohawk Trail, between Albany and Schenectady. It was a train of stagecoaches linked together, running on wooden tracks laid over granite blocks. The railroads were at first regarded as an addition to water routes. Many short, unconnected railroad lines, often built for different sized equipment, were constructed along the Mohawk Trail in the 1830s.

As they began to threaten trade on the state-controlled canal, railroads were blocked by the state. However, even with expansion of the canal, the freight passing through soon became more than it could handle. By 1851, railroads were growing and operating freely. The short railroad lines began to join together. Along the Mohawk River, they formed the New York Central Railroad. This railroad called itself "the only water level route to the West," and it ran close to the route of the Erie Canal. With the Erie Canal and the New York Central Railroad in place, a great deal of the long-distance freight from the expanding West moved along the Mohawk Trail. New York City became the trade and financial center of the nation.

The Demise of the Turnpikes. With the arrival of the railroad, the turnpike system was finished. Even the best of the turnpike companies had paid only small dividends to their stockholders. Many had been on the edge of bankruptcy from the beginning, because of the high cost of maintaining the roads. They made one last bid for life. In the 1840s, Russian-style plank roads began to be built in the timber-rich country along much of the Mohawk Trail. Planks eight feet wide were placed sidewise over beams buried lengthwise in the earth. Usually, only the more heavily traveled side of the turnpike was planked. Planked roads could carry heavier loads and were passable no matter what the weather, but the planks decayed quickly and the roads became dangerous. After that, both plank roads and ordinary turnpikes declined and were given to the state government by their bankrupt companies.

By 1871, only the easternmost 10 miles of the Great Western Turnpike leading into Albany was still run by a turnpike company. Many taverns along the way were converted into private homes. The few remaining stagecoach lines survived by running connecting services between rural towns and the railroads and canals. They served that purpose for several decades, until automobiles became common. Towns along the turnpikes became isolated, backwater villages, except for the few that had become resorts. Some, along the Finger Lakes, or those with mineral springs, attracted vacationers from New England and southern New York.

MODERN TIMES

The railroad had a further impact on the Mohawk Trail. Once engineers had the ability to cross mountains with ease, the sea-level original route lost some of its natural advantage. Goods and people, including millions of immigrants from Europe, still passed through the Mohawk Cut on the New York Central Railroad. Luxury express trains like the Twentieth Century Limited and the Empire State Express set speed records along the level route from New York to Chicago. However, other east-west routes through the mountains, even though they could not match the New York Central's speed, began to take a larger share of the traffic.

The Erie Canal in the 20th Century. The Erie Canal, too, lost its importance in the face of this shift to the railroad and away from the Mohawk route. New York State revived the Erie Canal in the early 20th century by making it nearly twice as wide and rerouting parts of it. In the east, it made the north side of the Mohawk River itself a canal. In the west, the canal went north of Syracuse, before rejoining the old route.

The new canal was completed in 1918 and became part of the State's Barge Canal System. It could take large ships carrying 2,500-ton loads. The ships could sail from distant Great Lake ports through to New York without reloading. Even so, the Erie Canal gradually lost ground to other routes. It still operated, carrying mostly grain and petroleum products. By the middle of this century, however, it was no longer important, especially after the opening of the St. Lawrence Seaway in 1959.

In the early 20th century, traffic began to travel over the Appalachians in many places, rather than through the original natural cut along the Mohawk River. New York City was still a key financial and trading center but was now the crossroads of many routes, not the end destination of just one.

The Automobile Age. The automobile era brought a new age of highways. The new paved highways—serving both local and long-distance needs—were often constructed on the old routes. Modern travelers driving on the Massachusetts Turnpike (Interstate 90) or riding the rail line from Boston to Albany follow roughly the route taken by early New Englanders moving west along the Mohawk Trail. Commuters on State Route 5 (State Street) between Albany and Schenectady are following the route of the old portage, along the Mohawk, before the Erie Canal cut a direct connection to the Hudson.

Drivers taking the old Mohawk Turnpike through the factory area on the north bank of the Mohawk River are following one leg of the original Mohawk Trail; the New York State Thruway (Interstate 90) follows the general line of the other leg for a while.

U.S. Route 20 has beautiful views along the ridge that edges the wide Mohawk Valley. Most tourists on it would be surprised to learn that they are following the shortcut route of the Great Western Turnpike. It later joins State Route 5 along the Great Genesee Road and other old routes all the way to Buffalo and Lake Erie.

Peter Wilson, chief of the Cayugas, clearly described the impact of history on the trails that began as footpaths through the Mohawk River Valley. Speaking to the New York Historical Society in 1847, he said:

> The Empire State, as you love to call it, was once laced by our trails from Albany to Buffalo; trails that we have trod for centuries; trails worn so deep by the feet of the Iroquois that they became your roads of travel, as your possessions gradually ate into those of my people. Your roads still traverse those same lines of communication which bound one part of the Long House to the other.

SUGGESTIONS FOR FURTHER READING

Flick, Alexander C., ed. *History of the State of New York*, in 10 volumes (New York: Columbia University Press, 1933-1935). An excellent resource, especially Volume V, which includes a short history of transportation in New York State.

Freedgood, Seymour, and the editors of Time-Life Books. *The Gateway States: New Jersey, New York* (New York: Time Inc., 1967). Part of the Time-Life Library of America. A handy historical overview of the area, with useful maps of the trails and routes at various stages.

Hislop, Codman. *The Mohawk* (New York: Rinehart & Co., Inc., 1948). Part of the Rivers of America series. A popular history of the trails and waterways of the Mohawk Valley.

Hulbert, Archer B. *Historic Highways of America*, in 17 volumes (Cleveland, Ohio: Arthur H. Clark Co., 1902-1905). Described by the author as "a collection of monographs of varying quality written with youthful enthusiasm by the author, who traversed in good part the main pioneer roads and canals of the eastern portion of the United States."

The Paths of Inland Commerce: A Chronicle of Trail, Road, and Waterway (New Haven: Yale University Press, 1920). An attractive overview of the development of human pathways in the eastern United States.

Jameson, J. Franklin, ed. *Narratives of New Netherland, 1609-1664* (New York: Barnes & Noble Books-Imports, 1967). A collection of early accounts.

Wright, Louis B., and Elaine W. Fowler, eds. *The Moving Frontier* (New York: Delacorte Press, 1972). This is an account of North America as seen through the eyes of its pioneer discoverers.

Writers' Program of the Works Project Administration in the State of New York. *New York: A Guide to the Empire State* (New York: Oxford University Press, 1940). Part of the American Guide series, this is a fine source of interesting historical detail for travelers.

2

THE WILDERNESS ROAD AND OTHER TRANS-APPALACHIAN ROUTES

In northeastern North America, the Mohawk Trail was a natural route across the Appalachian Mountains and into the center of the continent. As the European settlement of North America continued, additional, more southern, paths through the mountains became necessary. These routes served pioneers who settled the lands that would become Kentucky, Tennessee, Ohio, Indiana, and other states in the Mississippi River Basin, and the building of the trans-Appalachian routes marked a critical turning point in the westward expansion of the young United States of America.

OBSTACLES TO TRANS-APPALACHIAN ROUTES

Routes across the Appalachians took a long time to develop because the geography of the area and the politics of the time discouraged western exploration for many years. The geography is very simple: the Appalachian Mountains run from mid- Georgia in the south all the way to Canada. They form a natural barrier between the plains of the east coast and the plateaus and rivers to the west, facing the great Mississippi River Basin. There were openings through the mountains, but not many, and what openings there were, were difficult for early travelers to cross.

The French. Even when geographical difficulties could be over-
come, the political struggles for control of North America slowed
down exploration. The earliest British settlements in North America were in a narrow strip between the east coast and the Appalachians, from Maine to southern Georgia. French settlements were
wrapped around these British colonies.

The French explorers claimed the Mississippi River Valley a
century before the British began to move across the Appalachian
Mountains. In the mid-1600s, the presence of the French to the west
often discouraged British exploration, as the experience of the
British Hunter-Salley party shows. This party explored west from
southern Virginia during the spring and summer of 1642. They
easily crossed the mountains to the Woods River, which runs into
the Ohio River. Once on the Ohio, they passed the falls of the Ohio
River, at what would later be Louisville, Kentucky.

There was no major natural barrier to travel all the way from the
falls of the Ohio to the mouth of the Mississippi River, a distance of
well over one thousand miles. However, just 300 miles upriver from
New Orleans, the party finally encountered a human obstacle:

> ...we were suddenly surprised by a company of men...to the number
> of ninety, consisting of Frenchmen, Negroes, and Indians, who took
> us prisoners and carried us to the Town of New Orleans, which was
> about one hundred leagues from us when we were taken, and after
> being examined upon oath before the Governor first separately one
> by one, and then all together, we were committed to close Prison...

They were imprisoned for two years before being allowed to return
home to Virginia. Ownership of the west had to be determined before
hundreds of thousands of pioneers could follow these early explorers
across the Appalachians and into the Mississippi Basin. Until then,
westward travel remained only a trickle.

The Native Americans. The French were not the only barrier to
British moves west. The Native Americans in the region also played
a part. In their battles with the French, the British formed alliances
with several Native American groups. In exchange for help from the
Native Americans, the British agreed to limit their settlements west
of the Appalachians. So it was that British colonists were penned
into the coastal plain of eastern North America for 150 years. Only
after winning the American Revolution were former colonists able
to push out across the Appalachians in great numbers, breaking

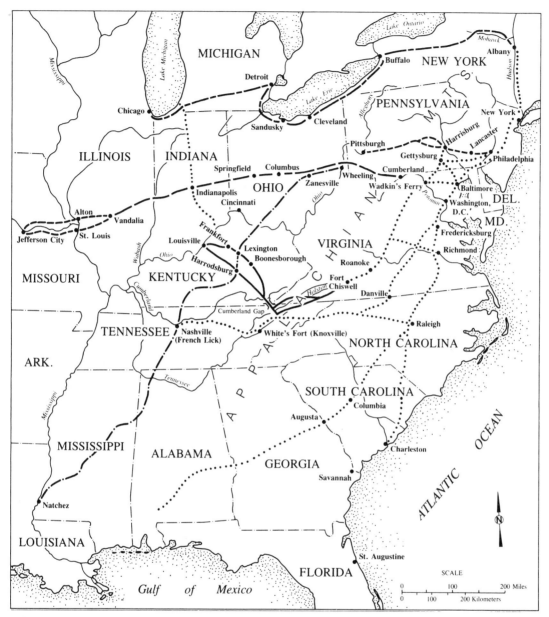

The Wilderness Road and Other Main Routes to the West in the Early 19th Century

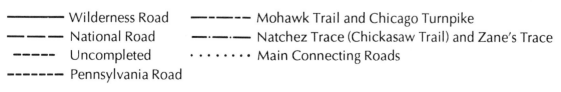

——————— Wilderness Road   ——————— Mohawk Trail and Chicago Turnpike

——·——·—— National Road   ——·——·—— Natchez Trace (Chickasaw Trail) and Zane's Trace

- - - - - - Uncompleted   · · · · · · · · Main Connecting Roads

- - - - - - - Pennsylvania Road

longstanding treaties between the British and Native Americans. The Americans then completed the journey of conquest west to the Pacific Ocean in less than half the time it had taken them to cross the Appalachians.

THE TRAILS

There were three main routes west across the Appalachian Mountains. The Wilderness Road ran from Virginia through the Cumberland Gap into Kentucky and Tennessee. Farther north the Pennsylvania Road went from Philadelphia across Pennsylvania, meeting the Ohio River in what later became the city of Pittsburgh. The National Road ran from Maryland to West Virginia, crossing the Ohio River near Wheeling. It then ran straight across what later became the states of Ohio, Indiana, and Illinois to St. Louis, Missouri, on the Mississippi River.

The river connections on these routes, especially the Ohio River, were very important. In the days when overland travel was long and hard, travelers took advantage of water routes whenever they could. The Ohio River and other west-flowing streams that fed into the Mississippi were easy routes west, once settlers had crossed the mountains.

Origins of the Routes. Early American travelers were not trailblazers. They usually followed trails laid down long ago. Native Americans had traveled the Appalachians for thousands of years before the European settlers came. Particularly important was an old network of Native American paths called the Warrior's Path. The Warrior's Path stretched all along the east slope of the Appalachian Mountain chain, from Iroquois country in upstate New York to Cherokee country in Georgia. These old paths also moved through and around the mountains, out into the Shawnee Indian country of western Tennessee, Kentucky, and Ohio.

The colonists' only real problems were caused by the heavy forest they had to move through. These mountain trails through thick forests were usable by people on foot or on horseback, but not by wagons or even light-wheeled carts.

Crossing the Cumberland Gap. In 1750, Dr. Thomas Walker crossed the Appalachian range, beginning near what is now Kingsport, Tennessee. He explored the land west of the mountains for a

London land company. It was he who first described Cave Gap, which became the main pass through the Cumberland Mountains and onto the plains of eastern Kentucky. He later called it Cumberland Gap, the name under which it passed into American history. His diary records the scene:

> April 13th. We went four miles to a large creek, which we called Cedar Creek, being a branch of Bear-Grass, and from thence six miles to Cave Gap, the land being level....On the south side is a plain Indian road. The mountain on the north side of the gap is very steep and rocky, but on the south side it is not so. We called it Steep Ridge. At the foot of the hill on the north west side we came to a branch [small creek], that made a great deal of flat land. We kept down it two miles, several other branches coming in to make it a large creek, and we called it Flat Creek. We camped where we found very good coal. I did not see any lime stone beyond this ridge. We rode 13 miles this day.

The "plain Indian road" Walker had discovered was part of the Warrior's Path. It ran from the Shawnee villages along the Scioto River, a feeder of the Ohio, south through the Cumberland Gap into the country of the Catawbas and Cherokees. Large stretches of it became part of the Wilderness Road.

Early Development of the Wilderness Road. Key figures in the development of the Wilderness Road were Daniel Boone and land speculator Colonel Thomas Henderson. In the early spring of 1775, Colonel Henderson and Daniel Boone met with leaders of the Cherokee nation. They met at Sycamore Shoals, on the Watauga River, near where Tennessee, North Carolina, and Virginia meet today. Here, for some thousands of pounds worth of goods and 2,000£ (British currency) in cash, these Cherokees "sold" Henderson most of Kentucky and other land beyond the Appalachian Mountains. What Henderson "bought" was all the land south of the Ohio River between the Cumberland and Kentucky rivers. It was a huge area of about 20 million acres, and included a right of way through the Cumberland Gap.

The son of one of the Cherokee chiefs was a young man named Dragging-Canoe. He spoke strong against the sale, and later told Boone:

> You have bought a fair land, but there is a cloud hanging over it. You will find its settlement dark and bloody.

This view of Cumberland Gap, in the late 19th century, shows both Daniel Boone's road and a later, straighter military road through the same gap. (Etching by Harry Fenn, from *Picturesque America*, New York, 1872)

These are much-quoted words and proved to be a good prediction, though the worst sufferers in the long run were the Cherokees themselves.

The Governor of Virginia, Lord Dunsmore, called the Henderson purchase illegal. It was seriously questioned by many in the southern colonies, including George Washington. But the main result of the Cherokees' sale of this land was the opening of what became the Wilderness Road.

BUILDING THE WILDERNESS ROAD

Henderson used Daniel Boone and his party of 30 axmen to clear a road through the Cumberland Gap and into Kentucky. On March 10, 1775, they started west from the place where the Great Philadelphia Wagon Road met the Holston River. They mainly followed Native American paths and buffalo tracks and did a very small amount of path-straightening and brush-clearing on the way.

Boone's party pushed through the Cumberland Gap and then joined the Warrior's Path and followed it for about 20 miles. They left the old trail and cut a path through the woods out of the mountains and onto low, rolling Kentucky country, headed for the Kentucky River. Near what is now Richmond, Indiana, their poorly guarded camp was successfully attacked by Shawnees. Fortunately for Boone, the Shawnees did not follow up their attack. The Boone party was able to reach the Kentucky River and set up camp there. Later that year, they were joined by Henderson and a much larger group of settlers. Together they founded the town of Boonesborough.

Here is Boone's version of what happened:

> I undertook to mark out a road in the best passage from the settlement through the wilderness to Kentucke. I soon began this work, having collected a number of enterprising men, well armed. We proceed with all possible expedition until we came within fifteen miles of where Boonsborough now stands, and where we were fired upon by a party of Indians that killed two, and wounded two of our number; yet, although surprised and taken at a disadvantage, we stood our ground. This was on the 20th of March, 1775. Three days after that we were fired upon again, and had two men killed, and three wounded. Afterwards we proceeded on to Kentucky river without opposition; and on the first day of April began to erect the fort of Boonsborough at a salt lick, about sixty yards from the river, on the south side.

The Final Destination. Benjamin Logan traveled with the Henderson party. He split off south of Boonesborough at Hazel Patch, traveling west on the route that would complete the main line of the Wilderness Road, through what would be Harrodsburg. Later travelers pushed the Wilderness Road a little farther, to its end at the falls of the Ohio River, at Louisville, Kentucky.

Geographer Ellen Churchill Semple well describes the web of trails together known as the Wilderness Road.

> The Cumberland Gap route was the natural avenue to the West for emigrants from Virginia and the Carolinas, but it was preferred also by colonists from Philadelphia when they carried little baggage, through the distance from that city to the interior of Kentucky was eight hundred miles. From Philadelphia an established line of travel led across the Potomac by Wadkin's Ferry, and up the Valley of Virginia [part of the Great Valley of the Appalachians] along the old war-trail of the Iroquois and Cherokee, over the low watershed to the New River. The pioneers crossed that stream and continued up its western affluent [feeder], Reed Creek, which on an almost level divide interlocks with the head streams of the Holston. Here the western trail was joined by another path from Richmond, Virginia, and here at the "forks of the road" was Fort Chissel, the block-house built in 1758 to hold the Cherokees in check. At this point began the Wilderness Road. The distance to Cumberland Gap was two hundred miles.

At the upper part of the Holston River, the Wilderness Road turned west and crossed several parallel mountain ranges. At the Powell River, the trail turned down the valley to the Cumberland Gap, "which opened an easy gateway through the Cumberland Mountains to the West." Beyond the pass, the trail joined the Warrior's Path. Semple continues:

> The Wilderness Road, as tracked in 1775, by Daniel Boone for Colonel Henderson, followed this Indian trail across the ford of the Cumberland, where this river breaks through Pine Mountain, and down the stream for a few miles to Flat Lick; but here it turned northwest, and followed a buffalo trace along the ridges over to Rockcastle River. From the Rockcastle River, the road went north along the Kentucky River through Boonesborough, then on to Lexington and, as Semple says, "the smiling lands of the Bluegrass."

A second branch of the Wilderness Road also began at the Rockcastle River. This branch "turned northwest and, by a natural gateway near Carb Orchard, reached level land near the present town of Stanford..." Eventually, this branch of the road became more important than the northern branch. It led "directly to the attractive level lands of Kentucky, and, passing through Danville, Bardstown, and Bullitt's Lick, terminated at the Falls of the Ohio [Louisville]." From Louisville a traveler could easily do business with the trading posts that had grown up on the Mississippi and Wabash rivers.

Travelers could also use the Wilderness Road as a route to Tennessee. After passing through the Cumberland Gap, another trail turned southwest and went to the "bend of the Cumberland," where Nashville was established. For westbound travelers, the Cumberland Gap had become a well-used passage through the mountains.

Emigrants on the Wilderness Road. The Wilderness Road proved to be a very good way west for emigrants from Virginia and the Carolinas, and from as far north as Philadelphia. After the Revolution, by 1792, when Kentucky became a state in the new United States, about 70,000 people had poured west through Cumberland Gap. They were soon joined by many more.

Some came out of Philadelphia directly west through Pennsylvania. Others pushed across New York's Mohawk Trail and then turned south to the Ohio. By 1800, the population of Kentucky was 221,000. Ten years later, it had reached 407,000. By the early 1780s, emigrants were also crossing south of the Cumberland Gap, on the Tennessee Path, out to Nashville and beyond, to the Mississippi. By 1820, Kentucky and Tennessee had a population of 1 million people, one-tenth of the country's total population of nearly 10 million. The move west across the mountains had formed a huge population shift for the new American nation.

THE PENNSYLVANIA ROAD

After the Revolution, emigrants from the mid-Atlantic States began to head more directly west. The main goal of those headed west from Philadelphia was Pittsburgh where the Allegheny and Mononga-hela rivers join to form the Ohio River. From late in the 18th century until late in the 19th century, millions of people poured through Pittsburgh on the way west. Large cities were established, and much business traffic passed between them along the Pennsylvania Road. This route mainly follows the course of the modern U.S. Route 30. It runs from Philadelphia through Lancaster and through Harrisburg—the present state capital. Then it moves over the mountains into western Pennsylvania and on to Pittsburgh.

The Pennsylvania Road's eastern section, the Philadelphia and Lancaster Turnpike, was completed in 1796. It was one of the earliest gravel—rather than plain dirt or log—roads in the country. The western section was called Forbes Road, named after the

From this small settlement in 1796, Pittsburgh grew into a major city, as travelers funneled westward to the Ohio River. (From Victor Collot, *Atlas in Voyage dans l'Amerique Septentrionale*, 1826, New York Public Library)

In the days after the Revolution, this road pushed west from Baltimore, past the rough tavern shown in the left foreground. (From *Columbian Magazine*, Library of Congress)

British general who used it to supply his forces while taking Fort Duquesne (now Pittsburgh) from the French in 1758.

The Heyday of the Pennsylvania Road. From the mid-18th century, and especially during the first third of the 19th century, the Pennsylvania Road carried a great volume of vehicles. Over it traveled everything from the pack trains and light carts of the early period to the big Conestoga freight wagons and swift express stagecoaches of later times. When railroads and the Pennsylvania Canal were built later in the 19th century, however, the western section of the Pennsylvania Road was little used, and the eastern sections carried mostly local traffic.

THE NATIONAL ROAD

Another important route west flourished for a short time during the first half of the 19th century. This was the National Road, also called the National Pike or the Cumberland Road. It mainly followed the route of what is now U.S. Route 40 from Cumberland, Maryland, through Wheeling, West Virginia. Then it went west through southern Ohio, Indiana, and Illinois to meet the Mississippi at St. Louis. The National Road carried a large volume of traffic during the American push west. It also formed the first major federal interstate highway in America.

Demand for a New Road. By the turn of the 19th century, settlers headed west were putting great pressure on the new federal government to build a major road from the east that would link the Atlantic coast and the Mississippi. In response, the federal government voted in 1806 to build the National Road. The first building contracts were granted in 1811, and the earliest section of the road was completed in 1818. It was a 30-foot-wide road on an 80-foot-wide right of way from Cumberland to Wheeling. The road was well-constructed, and Thomas B. Searight, early historian of the National Road, noted that:

> Its numerous and stately stone bridges, with handsome, turned arches, its iron mileposts, and its old iron gates, attest to the skill of the workmen engaged on its construction...

The building of the National Road was of great importance for the American move west. Wheeling is on the Ohio River, and many emigrants and traders took the National Road to Ohio where they exchanged wagons for flatboats. They then used these boats to continue west by river.

The part of the National Road near Wheeling was very popular with travelers. Searight observed traffic on the road during its heyday:

> As many as twenty four-horse coaches have been counted in line at one time on the road, and large, broad-wheeled wagons, covered with

Day and night the Conestoga wagons thundered along the National Road in Pennsylvania in the 1830s. (By C. W. Jefferys, from Archer B. Hulbert, *The Paths of Inland Commerce,* 1921)

white canvas stretched over bows laden with merchandise and drawn by six Conestoga horses were visible all the day long at every point, and many times until late in the evening, besides innumerable caravans of horses, mules, cattle, hogs and sheep. It looked more like a leading avenue of a great city than a road through rural districts...

For people living along this busy road, traffic provided a form of entertainment. Searight wrote:

Excitement followed in the wake of the coaches all along the road. Their arrival in the towns was the leading event of each day, and they were so regular in transit that farmers along the road knew the exact hour of their coming without the aid of watch or clock. They ran night and day alike.

Searight also described how great distances were covered on the National Road in as little time as possible:

Relays of fresh horses were placed at intervals of twelve miles as nearly as practicable...Teams were changed almost in the twinkling of an eye. The coach was driven rapidly to the station, where a fresh team stood ready harnessed waiting on the roadside. The moment the team came to a halt the driver threw down the reins and almost instantly the incoming team was detached, a fresh one attached, the reins thrown back to the driver, who did not leave his seat, and away again went the coach at full speed.

Delays During Construction. This first section of the National Road ran 131 miles from Cumberland to Wheeling and was heavily used. Political troubles delayed the building of the much longer second section of the road. This section ran 530 miles from Wheeling to St. Louis, Missouri. The road was completed as far as Columbus, Ohio, in 1833, a full 15 years after it had reached Wheeling. It did not reach Vandalia, then the Illinois state capital, until 1852, long after the major migrations to the west had taken place. As a result, later sections of the National Road served local traffic more than national traffic. The route did, however, set the locations of several midwestern cities, including Columbus, Ohio, and Indianapolis, Indiana.

The Routes in Decline. By the 1850s, the great days of the Wilderness Road and the Pennsylvania Road were over. By this time, the Mississippi River Valley had long been settled. Americans had already started the great movement west from the Mississippi

and the Missouri along the Oregon and California Trails. Railroads and canals had been built, which took the place of the roads for both trade and long-distance traffic.

The Wilderness Road, the Pennsylvania Road, and the National Road were used only for relatively short periods of time. Yet these routes had a huge and lasting importance, for these were the roads that first took the people of the new United States over the mountains into the heart of North America and helped further the settlement of the continent.

By the mid-20th century, the Appalachians were crossed by great highways, traveled by trucks like this one, refueling at night at the modern Pennsylvania Turnpike. (May 1945. Records of the Bureau of Public Roads; 30-N-47-90-C)

SUGGESTIONS FOR FURTHER READING

Billington, Ray Allen. *The Westward Movement in the United States* (New York: Van Nostrand Reinhold, 1959). A useful general history of American westward movement from sea to sea.

Cumming, W. P., et al. *The Exploration of North America* (New York: Putnam's, 1974). A large, heavily illustrated work, containing a good deal of material quoted from early explorers.

De Voto, Bernard. *The Course of the Empire* (Boston: Houghton, Mifflin, 1952). A full history of the exploration and conquest of North America.

Dunbar, Seymour. *History of Travel in America* (New York: Bobbs-Merrill, 1915). A full early history of travel in the United States, from colonial times through the completion of the first transcontinental railway.

Hulbert, Archer B. *The Paths of Inland Commerce* (New Haven: Yale, 1921). A classic short work on American trails, roads, and waterways.

Josephy, Alvin M. *The Indian Heritage of America* (New York: Knopf, 1969). An excellent general work on the history and culture of the Native Americans of the Americas.

Kincaid, Robert L. *The Wilderness Road* (New York: Bobbs-Merrill, 1947). A popular history of the Wilderness Road and related routes.

Merk, Frederick. *History of the Westward Movement* (New York: Knopf, 1978). A full history of the entire American westward movement from sea to sea.

Rose, Albert C. *Historic American Roads: From Frontier Trails to Superhighways* (New York: Crown, 1967). A brief popular work, with color paintings and maps.

Rouse, Park Jr. *The Great Wagon Road* (New York: McGraw-Hill, 1973). A detailed history of this road, with a section on the Wilderness Road.

Semple, Ellen Churchill. *American History and Its Geographic Conditions* (Boston and New York: Houghton Mifflin, 1903). A classic work on the influence of geography on patterns of development and settlement in the United States, with excellent maps.

Stewart, George R. *U.S. 40* (Boston: Houghton Mifflin, 1953). A detailed, section-by-section treatment of U.S. 40, from coast to coast; includes historical material on the National Road.

3

THE MISSISSIPPI ROUTE

THE "GREAT RIVER"

...the great Mississippi, the majestic, the magnificent Mississippi,
rolling its mile-wide tide along, shining in the sun...

This mighty river, as seen by Mark Twain in his *Life on the
Mississippi*, was surely well suited to occupy center stage in the
history of the settlement of North America. Its very name means
"great river." The Mississippi extends over 2,000 miles of the American heartland, from Minnesota in the north to the Gulf of Mexico
in the south. It links up with several other major rivers and scores
of smaller ones to form a system of over 15,000 miles of navigable
waterways.

This system of rivers has had significance in the history of the
North American continent. One thousand years before the birth of
Christ, Native Americans used the Mississippi River system to
travel and trade throughout the continent. When European explorers and settlers arrived, they used and expanded the Native American routes. As the push west continued, the amount of cargo and
passenger traffic on the rivers increased. Travel and trade on the
Mississippi reached their peak during the Steam Age of the 1880s,
when steam-powered boats carried all kinds of crops, manufactured
goods, livestock, and people up and down the river system. Today,
though other methods of transportation have caused a decrease in
river traffic, certain materials continue to be shipped by river, and
the Mississippi River system still acts as an important gateway into
North America.

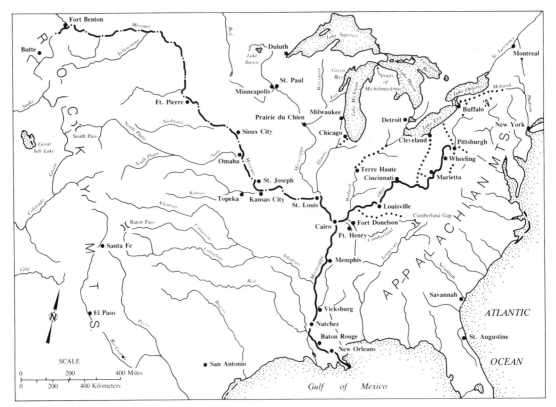

The Mississippi Route in the 1840s

———————— Main Mississippi Route   · · · · · · · · Main Canal Connections

—— · —— · —— Main Missouri Route

THE TRAIL

The Mississippi River system covers the heart of North America. The Mississippi itself flows from Lake Itasca, northwest of Duluth, Minnesota, to the Gulf of Mexico, a distance of almost 2,400 miles. The system also includes the Missouri River, which flows 2,500 miles from Grand Forks, Montana, to its junction with the Mississippi, a little north of St. Louis. The third great river in the system is the Ohio. Beginning at Pittsburgh, the Ohio flows almost 1,000 miles west to its junction with the Mississippi at Cairo, Illinois. Each of these major rivers is fed by dozens of smaller rivers and streams that form an interconnected system of waterways extending over 15,000 miles.

From the north, the Mississippi system provides easy passage from the St. Lawrence and Great Lakes to the Gulf of Mexico. Going east to west on the Ohio and then the Missouri, the system provides an easy water passage from Pittsburgh to western Montana. There it links up with the Columbia River system.

The Mississippi system provided most of the main early routes west across the continent. People forged land routes out of the valleys cut by the rivers. In the East, the Ohio, Tennessee, and Cumberland rivers provided routes through and beyond the Appalachians. West of the Mississippi, explorers, trappers, traders, and then settlers followed by Missouri, Platte, Kansas, Arkansas, and Red (Colorado) rivers across the plains to the Rockies, and beyond to the Pacific.

Native Americans and the Mississippi Basin. The history of life and trade on the Mississippi began long before the arrival of Europeans. Native Americans were farming, trading, and creating artwork on the Mississippi a thousand years before Christ was born. Trade on the Mississippi, the Missouri, the Ohio, and many of the other streams and rivers that make up the huge Mississippi system had probably gone on for many years before that. The oldest surviving records of these activities describe a continent-wide trading network that extended from the Appalachian Mountains and the

These Mandan women, descendants of the great Mississippi Valley cultures, are gathering driftwood from the river for fuel, to be taken to their village, high on a bluff overlooking the river. (Engraving after a drawing by Charles Bodmer, from Maximilian, Prince of Wied Nu-Wied, *Travels in the Interior of North America in 1832-4*) southern Atlantic coast to the Rocky Mountains, and from the Gulf of Mexico to the Great Lakes and the high northern plains.

The Hopewell Culture. As early as the first century B.C., the Hopewell culture (named after the modern owner of the land containing one of their burial sites in Ohio) arose in the valleys of the Ohio, the Illinois, and the lower Mississippi rivers. The huge mounded burial sites that the Hopewell culture left behind show that these Native American farmers and hunters were also the great North American traders of their day. They used the waterways of the Mississippi Basin—and beyond—to get such things as grizzly bear teeth from the Rockies, conch shells from the Gulf of Mexico, mica from the southern Appalachians, and copper from the Great Lakes.

The Hopewell culture was replaced by other Native American cultures in the period 500-700 A.D., and widespread trading continued. The French and Basque fishermen who followed early explorer John Cabot to the shores of the New World after 1497 found Native Americans, ready to trade, on shore. The trade of European tools and other goods for furs was well established even before Cartier entered the Gulf of St. Lawrence in 1541.

Europeans "Discover" the Great River. The same year that the French explorer Jacques Cartier entered the Gulf of St. Lawrence in the north, Hernando De Soto of Spain "discovered" the Mississippi River. He and his party crossed it near what is now Memphis, Tennessee. They were traveling overland from Florida, in the third year of a four-year journey that took them all the way to what is now Texas. A year later, De Soto became ill and died somewhere on the lower Mississippi. De Soto and his party were seeking gold. They found none and went away, not knowing that they were leaving behind the key to the opening of a continent.

In *Life on the Mississippi*, Mark Twain shares his thoughts about the reaction of De Soto's party to the great river:

> De Soto merely glimpsed the river, then died and was buried in it by his priests and soldiers. One would expect the priests and the soldiers to multiply the river's dimensions by ten—the Spanish custom of the day—and thus move other adventurers to go at once and explore it. On the contrary, their narratives, when they reached home, did not excite that amount of curiosity. The Mississippi was left unvisited by

For 130 years after De Soto visited the Mississippi, Europeans left the great river unexplored. (Engraving after painting by W. H. Powell, New-York Historical Society)

whites during a term of years which seems incredible in our energetic days.

Twain goes on to discuss the length of time that passed before another European saw the Mississippi. He describes the interval by comparing it with the lifetime of another famous writer:

...after De Soto glimpsed the river, a fraction short of a quarter of a century elapsed, and then Shakespeare was born; lived a trifle more than half a century, then died; and when he had been in his grave considerably more than half a century, the *second* white man saw the Mississippi. In our day we don't allow a hundred and thirty years to elapse between glimpses of a marvel...

Like other Europeans of their time, the Spanish were seeking a passage to the Cathay (Marco Polo's word for China) and the Spice Islands. But they were intent on finding a passage through Central America. This left the Mississippi to other Europeans, starting with the French. The French had been active in exploring Canada from the time of Cartier's first explorations in 1541. However, it was 130 long years before another French explorer, La Salle, finally journeyed to the mouth of the Mississippi.

The first of the French explorers to reach the Mississippi were Louis Jolliet and Father Jacques Marquette in 1673. Twenty-nine years earlier, in 1634, Jean Nicolet had explored the Great Lakes country as far west as Green Bay, in modern Wisconsin, on the western shore of Lake Michigan, but Nicolet had not realized how close he then was to the great river. Jolliet and Marquette went farther. Traveling west from the French outpost at Michilimackinac, at the western end of Lake Huron, they entered Lake Michigan and followed Nicolet's route to Green Bay. Going west on the Fox River, they were then guided by local Native Americans on the old and well-used path between the Fox and Wisconsin rivers. Overland connections like these were called *portages*, from the French verb *porter*, meaning "to carry," for here travelers had to drag or carry their canoes over land from one waterway to another. Once on the Wisconsin, Jolliet and Marquette had entered the Mississippi River system. They were then able to take the Wisconsin River directly into the Mississippi, which they entered on June 17, 1673, near what is now Prairie du Chien.

First Glimpses of the Missouri and Ohio Rivers. The Jolliet and Marquette party, traveling in two birch-bark canoes, then followed the Mississippi south for almost a thousand miles. On the way, they passed the mouths of both the Missouri and Ohio. They turned back after reaching the mouth of the Arkansas River, at a point only about 400 miles north of the mouth of the Mississippi. Father Claude Dablon describes the first sighting—probably as told by Marquette—of the mouth of the Missouri, the river later known to Americans as "The Big Muddy":

> …sailing quietly in clear and calm water, we heard the noise of a rapid, into which we were about to run. I have seen nothing more dreadful. An accumulation of large and entire trees, branches, and floating islands, was issuing from the mouth of the river Pekitanoui [Missouri], with such impetuosity that we could not without great danger risk passing through it. So great was the agitation that the water was very muddy, and could not become clear.

He also wrote about what they hoped to find by exploring the river:

> Pekitanoui is a river of considerable size, coming from the northwest, from a great distance, and it discharges into the Mississippi. There

are many villages of savages along this river, and I hope by its means to discover the vermillion or California sea.

Judging from the direction of the course of the Mississippi, if it continues the same way, we think that it discharges into the Mexican Gulf. It would be a great advantage to find the river leading to the southern sea, toward California; and, as I have said, this is what I hope to do by means of the Pekitanoui, according to the reports made to me by the savages. From them I have learned that, by ascending this river for 5 or 6 days, one reaches a fine prairie, 20 or 30 leagues long. This must be crossed in a northwesterly direction, and it terminates at another small river, on which one may embark, for it is not very difficult to transport canoes through so fine a country as that prairie. This second river flows toward the southwest for 10 or 15 leagues, after which it enters a lake, small and deep, which flows toward the west, where it falls into the sea. I have hardly any doubt that it is the Vermillion Sea, and I do not despair of discovering it some day...

The French had no idea of the real distances involved. But this is a good description of the route from the Missouri, across the Continental Divide, to the Columbia River system and down to the Pacific. (The Continental Divide is the crest of the Rocky Mountains, dividing waters flowing to the Atlantic from those flowing to the Pacific.)

In 1682, Robert La Salle made the long journey from the Gulf of St. Lawrence to the mouth of the Mississippi River, becoming the first Frenchman to complete the trip. His goal was to expand an empire. La Salle claimed the Mississippi and its valley for France. He hoped to return to begin the building of a French colony there. It was not to be, either for La Salle or for France. He was killed by mutineers during his second trip to the Mississippi in 1687. The French soon lost the Mississippi Valley to the British, along with most of the remaining French areas of North America.

The Beginnings of Settlement on the Route. After La Salle, French travel and trade on the Mississippi began to develop, but slowly. In 1699, French coming south from the Great Lakes founded the outpost of Cahokia, across the river from what later became St. Louis. Cahokia had also been the largest center of the Native American Mississippians, containing their largest burial mounds. A year later, in 1700, Pierre le Moyne, Sieur d'Iberville, entered the Mississippi from the Gulf of Mexico. He founded the first French colony near the mouth of the river, and the European settlement of the lower Mississippi began.

Flat boats like these were common on American rivers before the age of the steamboat. (Mouth of the Missouri River about 1840, lithograph by John Caspar Wild, from *The Valley of the Mississippi Illustrated,* 1842, Lewis F. Thomas, ed.)

New Orleans was founded in 1718, and plantations began to be established upriver. By the mid-1700s, many French settlers and slaves were on the river. By 1770, there were about 13,500 French in Louisiana. However, the territory that La Salle had named Louisiana, after his patron, Louis XIV of France, was French for only a short time. After 1763, Britain took control of the land east of the Mississippi River. Spain held on to the land west of the Mississippi and the river itself, including the Mississippi delta, all still called Louisiana.

By the late 1700s, there was a good deal of traffic on the river. Materials such as cotton and furs were moved down the river by piroque (dugout canoe), keelboat (covered flat-bottomed boat), and flatboat (open barge). The trading of sugar cane, molasses, and rum had also begun. Boats sailed downstream easily, for they were running with the current. Return trips upstream were harder, especially with bulk cargo. They required hauling or poling boats against the current. As a result, the Mississippi did not become a fully used water route until later, when the age of steam power arrived, bringing with it powerful steamboats.

The Natchez Trace

Before steamboats arrived on the Mississippi, travelers and boat crews going north often avoided pushing upstream against the current by taking an overland route called the Natchez Trace. (*Trace* is an archaic word meaning "road.") The Natchez Trace ran about 450 miles, from Natchez on the Mississippi to Nashville on the Cumberland River. It was an old Native American trail, running partly through the country of the Cherokee, Choctaw, Chickasaw, and Natchez peoples. It has also been called the Chickasaw-Choctaw Trail, the Chickasaw Trace, the Nashville Road, and the Natchez Road.

In Spanish and French colonial times, the Natchez Trace had been a rough and dangerous trail for travelers. It had also been the scene of many battles between Native Americans and Europeans. The Chickasaws fought and defeated Hernando de Soto's Spanish explorers there in the 1540s. The Natchez people attacked the French settlements in Natchez territory in 1729. Then the Natchez themselves were almost destroyed by combined French and Chickasaw forces. Later the Chickasaws fought the French to a standstill.

After the American Revolution, the former British lands became part of the United States, and a huge tide of American settlers began to pour west over and around the Appalachian Mountains. By 1808, the Natchez Trace was a heavily used American frontier road and had been cleared and widened for use as a wagon road. However, it was a key road for only a short time. When steamboats came to the Mississippi, it became much easier to take the river both north and south. After that, the Natchez Trace was not often used as a route for long-distance travel. Instead, it became part of the web of local roads that served an ever-increasing number of local settlements.

AMERICANS GO WEST

By the 1820s, the United States was becoming established as a new nation, the cotton gin had been invented, and the steamboat had arrived on the Mississippi. The impact of these three events was enormous. After the American Revolution, the Mississippi River became the new country's western border. Only the delta remained Spanish, until 1800, when it went back to France for three years. After 1803, with the Louisiana Purchase, the Mississippi and much of the basin to the west was added to the United States.

The new Americans broke the British–Native American treaties that had kept settlers pinned to the East Coast, and an explosion westward from Atlantic to Pacific began. As early as the late 1780s, tens of thousands of Americans had undertaken migrations westward by raft, flatboat, and keelboat on the Ohio, Tennessee, and Cumberland rivers. Thousands more were going west by land on the Wilderness Road and the Natchez Trace. In 1788–89, over 800 boats went west past Fort Harmar (Marietta) on the Ohio, carrying 20,000 people, 7,000 horses, 3,000 cows, 900 sheep, and 600 wagons. By 1790, there were over 45,000 people in Ohio. Ten years later, the population had jumped to 230,000; by 1820, it had more than doubled that. By 1860, Ohio had almost 2.5 million people. In that year, the states of the Mississippi Basin held over 12.5 million people, almost 40% of the population of the United States.

The Cotton Gin Is Invented.   In the Mississippi Basin, the invention of the cotton gin had an important effect on the region's agriculture. Invented by Eli Whitney in 1793, the cotton gin was a machine that separated the cotton seeds from the cotton fiber. Less time was needed to clean the cotton, leading to an increase in the amount of cotton planted and produced. This increase, in turn, led to a larger demand for inexpensive ways to ship cotton and other materials on the river.

Steamboats Revolutionize Life on the Rivers.   In the 1850s, that demand was met by newly invented steamboats on the Ohio and lower Mississippi. Later, steamboats were adapted for use in the shallow waters of the middle and upper Mississippi and the Missouri as well.

Early steamboats like the *U. S. Explorer* were not very beautiful and sometimes downright ugly, with the boiler taking up most of the deck. (Lithographic engraving with Ives's report in 36th Congress, 1st session, *House Executive Doc. 90,* Serial 1058, 1861)

Throughout the history of the North American continent, waterways had been the main travel and trade routes into the American heartland. But now these routes became more important as an increasing number of farmers, fur traders, and planters sought quick routes over which to transport their goods. The rivers became huge, busy highways, and steam power provided a sure, easy, not-too-costly journey back upstream.

STEAMBOATING DAYS

The first steamboat on the Mississippi system was the *New Orleans*, a two-masted side-wheeler. It was launched at Pittsburgh, on the Ohio River, in March 1811, by Nicholas Roosevelt, Robert Fulton, and Robert Livingston, owners of the Ohio Steamship Navigation Company. Nicholas Roosevelt and his wife took the *New Orleans* on a journey that was the length of the Ohio and lower Mississippi. It was an eventful trip. Just after running the terribly difficult falls of the Ohio River, past Cincinnati, they were caught in the New Madrid earthquake, the most violent North American earthquake

The Mississippi was cotton country; these slaves are working in the cotton fields, with a steamboat on the river in the background. (From *History of the United States, 19th Century*)

of its time. Yet they and the *New Orleans* survived. At Natchez, they took on the first load of cotton to be carried by steamboat on the Mississippi. Arriving at New Orleans on January 12, 1812, their journey heralded a new age of travel and trade in the Mississippi Basin.

The Invention of the Shallow-Draft Steamboat.

Even though its first trip was a success, however, the *New Orleans* was not the kind of shallow-draft steamboat needed to travel much of the Mississippi Basin. The *New Orleans* needed a deep stream and could not travel from Pittsburgh to New Orleans and back during the drier seasons of the year. As a practical matter, boats like the *New Orleans* were limited to the deeper waters of the lower Mississippi, south of Natchez.

In 1816, Henry Shreve invented the first shallow-draft steamboat, the *Washington*. It was flat-bottomed and the engine and boilers were on deck. A second deck held cargo and people, and the pilothouse and two smokestacks sat high above all the rest. This was the shape of all the Mississippi Basin steamboats that were to follow. With steamboats traveling the river systems, the Ohio, Mississippi, and Missouri became busy emigrant highways, further opening up the continent.

This was when the great era of Mississippi Basin steamboating began. Big shallow-draft steamboats carried large numbers of people and huge amounts of cargo on the Ohio and Mississippi. Smaller steamboats, made for shallower water, could work on the Missouri all the way to Fort Benton, in northern Montana. They went to the Yellowstone country, and to the mouth of the Little Big Horn. The small northern river steamboats took supplies, settlers, traders, and soldiers north. They brought back furs, lead, soldiers, and in some periods, large amounts of gold and silver from the West.

The Danger of Piloting on the Mississippi.

Traveling the rivers was not easy, though, for there were always new dangers such as tree trunks to avoid, rockfalls, snags, and other obstacles. Also, the river shifted its course over time, so much so that most of the route down the Mississippi followed by La Salle in 1682 had become dry land just two centuries later.

Because the course of the river shifted so much, the job of the steamboat pilot was very risky. Pilots were admired and respected for their skill. Mark Twain is best known as the author of *The Adventures of Huckleberry Finn* and many other books. As a young man in the 1850s, though, Twain was a Mississippi River pilot. In

Life on the Mississippi, Twain shares with his readers some of the knowledge taught to him by a master pilot when Twain was an apprentice. The master, Mr. Bixby, teaches the student that the way the river *appears* is not necessarily the way the river *is*:

You see, this has got to be learned; there isn't any getting around it. A clear starlight night throws such heavy shadows that, if you don't know the shape of a shore perfectly, you would claw away from every bunch of timber, because you would take the black shadow of it for a solid cape; and you see you would be getting scared to death every fifteen minutes by the watch. You would be fifty yards from shore all the time when you ought to be within fifty feet of it. You can't see a snag in one of those shadows, but you know exactly where it is, and the shape of the river tells you when you are coming to it. Then there's your pitch-dark night; the river is a very different shape on a pitch-dark night from what it is on a star-light night. All shores seem to be straight lines, then, and mighty dim ones, too; and you'd better *run* them for straight lines, only you know better. You boldly drive your boat right into what seems to be a solid, straight wall (you knowing very well that in reality there is a curve there), and that wall falls

Led by the *Queen of the West,* these three side-wheelers—so called because the paddle is on the side—are rounding a bend in the Mississippi in 1866. (Currier & Ives, after F.F. Palmer, authors' archives)

back and makes way for you. Then there's your gray mist...You take a night when there's one of those grisly, drizzly, gray mists, and then there isn't *any* particular shape to a shore. A gray mist would tangle the head of the oldest man that ever lived. Well, then, different kinds of *moonlight* change the shape of the river in different ways. You see...you only learn the shape of the river; and you learn it with such absolute certainty that you can always steer by the shape that's *in your head*, and never mind the one that's before your eyes.

It was in this period—and largely thanks to Mark Twain—that the Mississippi began to take a unique place as a source of American folklore. There are enough stories and legends of the Mississippi to fill many books. For example, Twain told this story about the explorer Marquette, and the legendary Mississippi catfish:

A big catfish collided with Marquette's canoe, and startled him; and reasonably enough, for he had been warned by the Indians that he was on a foolhardy journey, and even a fatal one, for the river contained a demon "whose roar could be heard at a great distance, and who would engulf them in the abyss where he dwelt." I have seen a Mississippi catfish that was more than six feet long, and weighed two hundred and fifty pounds; and if Marquette's fish was the fellow to that one, he had a fair right to think the river's roaring demon was come...

The Mississippi in the Civil War. During the American Civil War, the Mississippi became more a battlefield and less an avenue of travel and trade. The Union wanted to control the river all the way to the Gulf in order to split the Confederacy. The Confederacy tried to hold the river while concentrating on fighting the war in the East. In a series of major battles during 1862, Union forces advanced from the north and south and took control of the entire river. They split the states west of the Mississippi from the Confederacy and laid much of the basis for the winning of the war. A Union fleet under the command of David G. Farragut took New Orleans in April 1862, and Union forces under the command of Ulysses S. Grant took Fort Henry on the Cumberland. Then Grant took Fort Donelson, on the Tennessee River, as well as the city of Memphis, Tennessee. Finally, Grant cleared the Mississippi in a series of battles ending with the taking of Vicksburg.

MODERN TIMES

The great days of Mississippi steamboating ended with the coming of the railraods. In the East, railroads began to carry traffic that would usually have traveled along the Ohio and other eastern rivers even before the Civil War. After the war, the huge American transcontinental railroad network grew, and travel and trade on the rivers declined. In the early 1880s, there was still much travel and trade on the Mississippi and Missouri. But the last steamboat left Fort Benton in 1890. By the early 1890s, the steamboating era was over throughout the Mississippi Basin.

There is still much commercial shipping on the Mississippi, the Ohio, the Missouri, and some of their feeder rivers. Such materials as coal, steel, iron ore, and lead can often be shipped more cheaply by water than by truck or railroad. This shipping continues to make New Orleans a major international port.

Some passenger ships have returned to the Mississippi Basin rivers, too. These are often rebuilt steamboats from the last century. They serve those for whom a steamboat trip on the Mississippi is a nostalgic and satisfying journey into a time and style that continues to hold fascination and appeal.

SUGGESTIONS FOR FURTHER READING

Banta, R. D. *The Ohio* (New York: Rinehart, 1949). Part of the Rivers of American series. A detailed work on the Ohio River.

Billington, Ray Allen. *The Westward Movement in the United States* (New York: Van Nostrand Reinhold, 1959). A concise, useful, general history of American westward movement from sea to sea.

Carter, Hodding. *The Lower Mississippi* (New York: Farrar & Rinehart, 1942). Part of the Rivers of America series. A full work on the history of the lower Mississippi River and its surrounding areas.

Caruso, John Anthony. *The Mississippi Valley Frontier* (New York: Bobbs-Merrill, 1966). A full, detailed history of the exploration and settlement of the Mississippi Valley by the French.

Clemens, Samuel (Mark Twain). *Life on the Mississippi* (H. O. Houghton, 1874). A classic work on the Mississippi and Missouri, with a brief historical introduction, and a main focus on life during the great era of steamboating.

Cummings, W. P., et al. *The Explorations of North America* (New York: Putnam, 1974). A large, heavily illustrated work, containing a good deal of material quoted from early explorers, accompanied by editorial commentary.

De Voto, Bernard. *The Course of Empire* (Boston: Houghton, Mifflin, 1952). A full history of the exploration and conquest of North America.

Donovan, Frank. *River Boats of America* (New York: Crowell, 1966). A good, detailed, popular survey of American river boats and boating.

Drago, Harry Sinclair. *Roads to Empire: The Dramatic Conquest of the American West* (New York: Dodd Mead, 1968). A brief history of most of the main American western trails; includes a section on steamboating on the Missouri.

Eifert, Virginia S. *Of Men and Rivers* (New York: Dodd, Mead, 1966). A full work on the history of United States rivers, focusing on steamboating era.

Hulbert, Archer B. *The Paths of Inland Commerce* (New Haven: Yale, 1921). A classic short work on American trails, roads, and waterways.

Josephy, Alvin M. *The Indian Heritage of America* (New York: Knopf, 1969). An excellent general work on the history and culture of the Native Americans of the North Americas.

Merk, Frederick. *History of the Westward Movement* (New York: Knopf, 1978). A detailed history of the entire American expansion, including the modern period.

Parkman, Francis. *La Salle and the Discovery of the Great West* (Boston: Little, Brown, 1897). Parkman's classic work on La Salle, his explorations, and his associates.

Semple, Ellen Churchill. *American History and Its Geographic Conditions* (Boston and New York: Houghton, Mifflin, 1903). A classic work on the influence of geography on the patterns of development and settlement in the Unite States, with excellent maps.

4

THE SANTA FE TRAIL AND THE CHIHUAHUA TRAIL

Immigrants from Asia set foot on the North American continent thousands of years ago. When they did, they began the history of the continent. These immigrants, who are known to us as Native Americans, blazed a system of trails that stretched from Alaska, south across the western prairies, through the length of Mexico and well into the continent of South America. Two important sections of this system became known as the Santa Fe Trail and the Chihuahua Trail.

MEXICO AND THE UNITED STATES

These trails were located in the region that covers what is now the southwestern United States and northern Mexico. Throughout its history, this area has experienced the development of great cultures and nations. The Santa Fe and Chihuahua trails provided these cultures with routes for war, hunting, and further migration. After the founding of the United States of America, the new nation expanded westward. The same trails that had once been used at first only by Native Americans and then European adventurers, became routes for the traders, settlers, and armies of the new nation. Some of what we think of when we hear the words "the old West"—the activities of cowboys, mountain men, gunslingers, etc.— occurred in the areas crossed by the Santa Fe and Chihuahua trails.

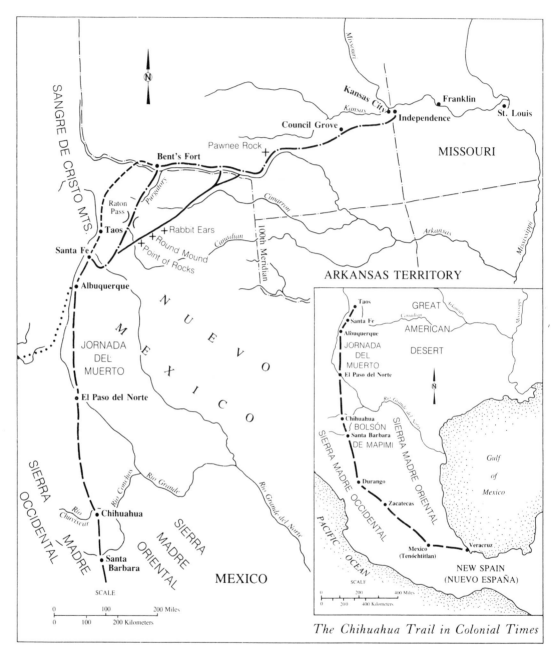

The Chihuahua Trail in Colonial Times

The Santa Fe Trail and the Chihuahua Trail in the 1830s

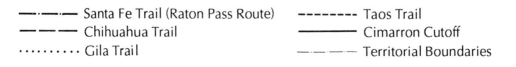

—·—·— Santa Fe Trail (Raton Pass Route)   - - - - - - - Taos Trail

— — — Chihuahua Trail   ——————— Cimarron Cutoff

·········· Gila Trail   —·—·— Territorial Boundaries

The region now contains the border between two nations—the United States and Mexico. Up until the early part of the 20th century, it was the site of border disputes between the two countries. To this day, the main travel routes between Mexico and the United States follow the general paths of the Santa Fe and Chihuahua trails.

THE TRAILS

Like two pieces of an arch, the Santa Fe Trail and the Chihuahua Trail reached toward each other. They bridged the open spaces between the Spanish colonies of the old Southwest and the settlements east of the Mississippi River. The Chihuahua Trail was by far the older of the two. Without it, there might have been no Santa Fe Trail. The younger trail grew in response to Santa Fe's needs and the aggressive trading military expansion of the United States. Even without that westward expansion, the Chihuahua Trail might today still be a major artery north to the Mexican colony of New Mexico—as important as it was at its beginning almost four centuries ago.

The Geography of the Chihuahua Trail. The Chihuahua Trail started in Mexico at Vera Cruz, on the Gulf of Mexico, and from there went to Mexico City. Then it continued north through central Mexico between the western and eastern mountain ranges, called the Sierra Madre Occidental and Sierra Madre Oriental. It crossed a dry, rugged plateau and went along the west side of a 500-mile-wide desert. This was the Bolsón de desert Mapimi, which extends up to the big bend of the great river of the north, the Rio Grande del Norte. The Chihuahua met the Rio Grande where the river turns due north and crossed the river at the narrow ford then called El Paso del Norte—now the city of El Paso, Texas. From there it followed the Rio Grande until just past present-day Albuquerque, where it left the river valley. Then it climbed northeast into the foothills of the Sangre de Cristo Mountains, part of the Rocky Mountains, to Santa Fe.

The Geography of the Santa Fe Trail. The Santa Fe Trail started in the heart of the continent. The Mississippi and Missouri rivers came together at St. Louis. From there, travelers could take the Missouri River west to Kansas City, where the Santa Fe Trail began as a path westward across the plains. Heading toward the Rocky Mountains, it followed the north side of the Arkansas River to the great bend in the river. Beyond that, the main route led into the Rockies, cutting south through Raton Pass and down into Santa Fe. A difficult shortcut went from the Arkansas River's great bend across the Cimarron Desert to Santa Fe. There, on the edge of the Rockies, the mountain chain that divides North America, it met the Chihuahua Trail.

EARLY TIMES

These routes passed through some of the longest settled country in the Americas. From Santa Fe through Mexico, the Chihuahua was part of the Great North Trail, the old migration route of the Native Americans that ran across the Bering Straight from Asia to Alaska and then south along the eastern slope of the Rockies all the way to Central America. Farther south, the migration route continued, following the line of South America's great Andes Mountains.

Many of the Native American settlers in the American Southwest lived in villages, some of them high up in cliffs or on top of mesas, like this one at Acoma, New Mexico. ("Acoma, No. 1," Lithographic engraving with Albert's report to the 30th Congress, 1st session, *House Executive Doc. 41*, Serial 517, Washington, 1848, National Archives)

The Pueblos. Many of the oldest cultures of North America flourished along the Great North Trail. The most notable of these were the Pueblo ("village") cultures in New Mexico. From a few centuries after the birth of Christ to the 14th and early 15th centuries, these cultures thrived. The reasons for their sudden collapse are not clear. Two possibilities are that they may have been victims of climate changes and that they may have been conquered by invaders. Some

of the Pueblo peoples vanished. They may have moved south to the Chihuahua area, where they became part of Mexico's Aztec culture. Aztec legend seems to support this possibility.

Other village-dwelling people also moved south, being pushed by nomads from the north. These newcomers called the cliff- and village-dwelling peoples "Anasazi," which means "the old ones." The Anasazi called the nomad-raiders "Apaches," or "the enemies." Some of the newcomers remained enemies of the Pueblo people. The Apaches and the Comanches, for example, continued raiding the Anasazis for centuries. Other invaders, such as the Navajos, inter- married with the Anasazis and adopted a settled life.

By the time the European settlers arrived, the southern section of the Chihuahua Trial was part of Aztec territory. The dry middle section was lightly populated by various peoples. The area north of El Paso was occupied by Pueblo peoples. And the Apaches and Comanches controlled the Santa Fe Trail.

The Spanish Invaders

Nuevo España. The modern history of the trails starts in the south. Less than 30 years after Columbus discovered the new world, the Spanish landed at the site of modern Vera Cruz, Mexico. They moved over 200 miles inland to take the Aztec capital of Tenóchtitlan, later renamed Mexico City. Then they swiftly took the dry plateau to the north, which they found to be studded with silver mines. By 1580, the colony of Nuevo España (New Spain) extended 850 miles north of Mexico City, to the Valle de San Bartolomé. It stopped at the Bolsón de Mapimi desert.

In this wild country, there were only a few widely scattered Spanish miners, soldiers, ranchers, and missionaries. Travel was unwise and unsafe except in large groups with military escort. A web of small trails crisscrossed the countryside, but most travelers used one north-south road that ran from Mexico City through Durango to Santa Barbara, at the time the northernmost town. This was the first and most important of the Mexican roads to be called El Camino Real—the Royal Road or the King's Highway.

Tales of gold to be found and "heathens" to be converted to Christianity inspired explorers and missionaries to try several routes farther north. To be sure of a supply of water, they went hundreds of miles out of the way, following a network of rivers. They even went so far west that they reached the Rio Grande by way of the Gila River Valley (today part of Arizona). These trips led to conflicts between the Spanish and Pueblo peoples. But no long-term settlements or routes resulted from these early forays.

Oñate's Caravan. The main direct route to the north was found in 1598 by Don Juan De Oñate, son of a wealthy silver miner. He was not the leader of an army or missionary expedition. Instead, he led a full-fledged, royally approved, emigrant party of about 200 people, 100 wagons, and 7,000 head of livestock. These people could hardly be cast in the stereotypical image of the plainly dressed, rough pioneer. Though they were headed for unknown country, they were dressed in the latest European styles. One nobleman in the caravan, for example, carried several suits, including some of satin, Italian velvet, and Chinese silk, all with the proper trimmings.

Traveling beyond the last settlement on El Camino Real, Oñate's caravan followed the edge of the Bolsón de Mapimi desert. The travelers camped at the last sure water source, the Rio Chuviscar. Then they headed straight north across the desert, following a trail blazed by an advance party. Although scarce water supplies would cause trouble for later travelers, this first party was lucky enough to experience a rare cloudburst, which left them with plenty of water. They wisely dropped some wagons along the way, to spare the load-bearing animals. In rugged country, they wound past mountain spurs through the valley of Encinillas over a narrow 5,300-foot pass. They skirted a large area of shifting sand dunes, called the Médanos. Finally they reached the Rio Grande just south of El Paso—"the pass."

The Caravan Moves Through El Paso. After more than two months on the road, Oñate held an official ceremony in which he took possession of the Rio Grande and surrounding area and named himself its governor. The party then moved up the west bank of the river through the narrow gorge to cross at the place still called El Paso. This part of the trail was very hard for wagons. They were guided by local Native Americans, who told them stories of ill-fated earlier explorers. The caravan then followed the east bank of the river to Robledo. Robledo was named for one of Oñate's traveling companions who died and was buried there.

Detour Through the Desert. At this point the river earns its alternate name, Rio Bravo del Norte—"rapid river of the north." It bends into a channel too narrow for wagons or even pack horses to cross. As a result, the travelers were forced to cross a 90-mile desert. Due to recent rain, Oñate's party crossed the desert easily, detouring to nearby mountain springs for water. Later travelers, without the benefit of rain, were forced to avoid the heat of day by making the crossing in three nighttime marches. They named the desert the Journada del Muerto, or "day's journey of the dead man," after someone who died trying to cross it in one day. Once across this desert the caravan again followed a twisting trail along the east bank of the Rio Grande, getting supplies from local Pueblos along the way. Five months after it began, Oñate's journey ended at a site he called Santo Domingo, 700 miles from the Rio Chuviscar. Oñate's trail, with only a few minor changes, became Mexico's central road of the north, El Camino Real. The northern part of this road was later famous as the Chihuahua Trail.

Settlement of the New Land. Once at the end of their trip, the travelers went their separate ways. The settlers started ranches in the river valley, and with some worry about their future in this new land, they set about their work. They were joined by other emigrant parties in the next few years. Sadly for Oñate, he did not find the rich mines that the Spanish government wanted. Nor was he a strong governor. He was removed from the post within a decade.

The Franciscan Friars. Indeed, the whole route would have been given up had it not been for the missionary Franciscan friars. They pleaded with the crown to support their missionary work and got their wish. A new governor was appointed, and at the turn of the year 1609–1610, he founded a new capital called Santa Fe— "holy faith." It was in a 7,000-foot-high valley in the Sangre de Cristo ("Blood of Christ") Mountains, 25 miles northeast of Oñate's first settlement. Of Santa Fe, trader Josiah Gregg noted:

> Like most of the towns in this section of country it occupies the site of an ancient Pueblo or Indian village, whose race has been extinct for a great many years. Its situation is…at the western base of a snow-clad mountain, upon a beautiful stream…of small mill-power size, which ripples down in icy cascades…

EARLY COLONIES

For the next 70 years, the settlers in Santa Fe and along the upper Rio Grande depended on a caravan service from Mexico City to provide goods that they could not produce themselves. The caravan was scheduled to make one round trip every three years. It was to spend six months on the road each way and six months distributing supplies and loading return goods. But sometimes it did not come for six or seven years. The route north was so dangerous that people traveling to the area for any reason usually awaited the arrival of the caravan so that they could travel with it. Over the decades, the wagon trail was used to move everything from mail and prisoners to trade goods. Although it was against the law to do so, officials often used the caravans to haul goods for their own private trading and personal profit. In fact, trade goods sometimes crowded out the mission supplies the caravan was supposed to carry.

Spanish Trade Monopoly. Spanish colonial policies also caused trouble in the area. As would be true until Spanish rule ended, all of New Spain's trade was controlled by Spanish government officials in Mexico City. The only official port for trading with Europe was Vera Cruz, on the east coast. Acapulco on the west coast was a much smaller trading port for goods going to and from East Asia. By having a monopoly, or exclusive control, on trade, the Spanish government drained wealth from its own colonies. Settlers' products were bought at low prices, but their supplies were costly. The settlers, therefore, made small profits, and the local economy suffered.

The Native Americans Revolt. Hardship among the Spanish settlers led to even greater hardship for the Native American peoples, who had been conquered and enslaved by the Spanish. Native Americans who had converted to Christianity and then gone back to their own religions were harshly punished. These conditions led to a revolt of the Pueblo peoples in 1680. Some 400 Spanish settlers were killed. The remaining 2,200 settlers retreated, mostly on foot, 330 miles back across the flood- swollen river at El Paso del Norte. One reason they survived was that emergency supplies from a special caravan reached them before they had to cross the Journada del Muerto. Many of the settlers chose to stay in the area. They formed a town on both sides of the river at El Paso.

The northern part of the Royal Road remained closed to the Spanish for 12 years. This was the case until the Native Americans were conquered again, this time by a new governor based at the site of modern Albuquerque. In 1693, some of the settlers from El Paso returned north. They drove their herds before them to trample down the brush and scrub that had grown over the trail. They were soon joined by new emigrants from central Mexico. The Spanish regained control of the whole area, this time for good. Santa Fe once again became the capital of New Mexico.

The Chihuahua Trail

In the same period, another important settlement was established. In 1697, near the Rio Chuviscar, where Oñate's caravan had camped, a mission called Nombre de Dios ("name of God") was founded. As Spanish settlers moved north into the colony of New Spain, many came to this key area. After 20 years and several name changes, the site came to be known as Chihuahua. In later decades, Chihuahua became the center of northern Mexico. It became a chartered city, a rich mining town, an army center, and a main trading center. In the early 1700s, though, the city was controlled from Mexico City.

The Caravan Service Resumes. With the resettlement of the province of New Mexico, north of El Paso, the caravan service to Santa Fe began again. But the schedule was still uncertain and the caravan's arrival and departure were announced only several days in advance by a town crier with drum and bugle.

As the northern population grew and the business importance of the caravan service increased, so its schedule became more settled. A regular, official trade fair was held in the old pueblo of Taos, in the hills 70 miles north of Santa Fe. This provided a fixed point of contact between Spanish merchants and the many Native Americans of the region. The caravan gradually set an annual schedule that brought merchants to Santa Fe in time for the Taos Fair, in July or August. By the mid-18th century, caravan service was no longer called a missionary supply operation, but rather a government one. As traffic on the Chihuahua Trail grew, unscheduled special-purpose caravans also operated.

The Dangers of the Trail. Travel on the Chihuahua Trail was far from safe. Caravans, regular or special, were always accompanied by army escorts. Regular troops manned presidios, or forts, in the main towns along the way. These towns included Chihuahua, El Paso del Norte, Albuquerque, and Santa Fe. To protect their livestock from the hostile Native Americans, ranchers often drove their herds along with the regular caravan. Some even hired special guards to go with them on their seasonal herd migrations. All male travelers with the caravans were expected to be armed, and their firearms were inspected before departure.

THE FRENCH TRADERS

As well as being a risky region in which to travel and live, New Mexico was a place where a settler was not likely to get rich. The continuing Spanish monopoly on trade drained wealth from the provinces. That caused the New Mexicans to become greatly interested in the new trade goods that began to reach their region from the East in the early 1700s.

English and French Colonies. In earlier times, when the Spanish were establishing royal roads in the Southwest, the English and French had had only small colonies in North America. The English settlements were strung out along the east coast of North America. English westward movement was blocked by the Appalachian Mountains, as well as by strong and active Native American tribes. Most of the French settlements were in the far northeast of the continent, but the St. Lawrence River brought them by a water route north of the Appalachians to the Great Lakes. From here, and from their other settlements at the mouth of the Mississippi River, they came into the heart of the country.

The goods that began to interest the New Mexicans in the early 1700s came from French traders. At first they came indirectly. French traders in Louisiana sold goods to some Pawnee Indians, who traded them to some Comanches, who brought them to the Taos Fair.

The Mallet Brothers. The first two French traders in the region, Paul and Pierre Mallet, arrived in 1739. The Mallets' arrival, like that of the caravans, was announced by the town crier. They were at first greeted warmly, especially since their goods were many times cheaper than similar goods coming from the south. However, the Spanish viceroy, or governor, in Mexico City forbade trading with the French, and these first traders were sent home. Later traders were jailed. Some were even sent as prisoners to Mexico City and held for years.

A New Trading Route Is Surveyed. As long as this Spanish trade policy was unchanged, there was no reason to carve out a route from the Mississippi River to Santa Fe. However, when the province of Louisiana was transferred from France to Spain in 1762, the New Mexican governor needed to review the choices of the most efficient route for Spanish goods. The cost of shipping goods overland 1,600 miles from Vera Cruz through Mexico City to Santa Fe made many items far too expensive. The Rio Grande could be navigated only by small boats, and it was often too shallow or dry for even that. There was no way to shorten the overland route from the south, even if the Spanish had allowed it. The New Mexicans thought they might ship goods first by water to the Mississippi, and then overland, from perhaps St. Louis, Missouri, or Natchitoches, Louisiana, so the governor of New Mexico had a French trader survey the route from

Zebulon Pike was one of several traders arrested on the road to Santa Fe and held for a time in a Mexican jail. (Painting by Charles Willson Peale, in Independence Hall, Philadelphia)

Santa Fe to the Mississippi. The survey was made in 1792–93. It marked out on paper the general route later known as the Santa Fe Trail. But the Spanish authorities would not let the route be used.

In 1800, Louisiana was returned to France, and in 1803 it was sold to the United States. American traders, some of French descent, began to trickle along the trail to Santa Fe, but they met with the same arrest and jailing that had faced earlier traders.

Zebulon Pike Makes Notes of the Trail. Zebulon Pike was a trader who was duly taken in charge by the New Mexicans. They tried to keep him from making notes about the sky and land as they took him on the Chihuahua Trail. But Pike outwitted them. After being warned not to take notes, he

> made a pretext to halt—established my boy as a vedette [lookout], and sat down peaceably under a bush and made my notes...This course I pursued ever after, not without some very considerable degree of trouble to separate myself from the party.

These notes formed the basis for a widely read report, and, as a result, American traders became more interested in the possibilities of trade in the region.

The American Traders

The Spanish trade monopoly continued until 1821. In that year, the Mexicans won their independence from Spain. The Mexicans now welcomed trade with the Americans, who could supply much-needed goods. That same year, traders from several points in Missouri headed for Santa Fe with their pack trains. The first was William Becknell. Some, like Becknell, followed river and mountain trails that they had learned about while trading with Native Americans.

These trips were so successful that some traders returned the following year. Indeed, several trappers and traders who crossed the plains toward Missouri in the summer of 1822 were astonished to see wagon tracks on the plains. These tracks were made by wagons belonging to Becknell, and were the first wagon tracks ever cut into southwest prairies.

The American Caravans. To the people living in Santa Fe, the arrival of an American caravan from Missouri was a great event.

Santa Fe trader Josiah Gregg described the scene in his classic chronicle, *Commerce of the Prairies*:

> To judge from the clamorous rejoicings of the men, and the state of agreeable excitement which the muleteers [mule handlers] seemed to be laboring under, the spectacle must have been as new to them as it had been to me. It was truly a scene for the artist's pencil to revel in. Even the animals seemed to participate in the humor of their riders, who grew more and more merry and obstreperous [hard to manage] as they descended towards the City. I doubt, in short, whether the first sight of the walls of Jerusalem were beheld by the crusaders with much more tumultuous and soul-enrapturing joy. The arrival produced a great deal of bustle and excitement among the natives. *"Los Americanos!"*—*"Los carros!"*—*"La entrada de la caravana!"* were to be heard in every direction; and crowds…flocked around to see the new-comers.

Increased Trade on the Trails. Caravans were not new to Santa Fe—they had been traveling north from Mexico through Chihuahua for over 200 years, on the Chihuahua Trail. What were new were the Americans and the inexpensive goods they brought. When Santa Fe was a frontier outpost of Mexico, what little there was of value in the area was taken for Spain. With Spain no longer controlling the region, the Americans began to see Santa Fe as an oasis in the "Great American Desert" of the Southwest. The Santa Fe Trail grew, and the Chihuahua Trail prospered out of the mutual desire of New Mexicans and Americans for contact and trade.

Becknell's Journey Through the Cimarron Desert. Although there were great new opportunities for trade, the life of a trader was not easy. On one of his return trips to Missouri, William Becknell blazed a trail across the Cimarron Desert. This was a dry basin drained by the often-waterless Cimarron River, which ran between the Canadian and Arkansas rivers. On the Cimarron crossing, Becknell's party found that water was the main problem. Their small canteen supply ran out in two days. Joseph Gregg reports:

> …the sufferings of both men and beasts had driven them almost to distraction. The forlorn band were at last reduced to the cruel necessity of killing their dogs, and cutting off the ears of their mules, in the vain hope of assuaging their burning thirst with the hot blood. This only served to irritate the parched palates, and madden the senses of the sufferers.

This is an artist's view of life in the "Great American Desert," before settlers and irrigation turned it into productive farm and ranch land. (*Harper's Weekly Magazine*, vol. XVI, no. 791, 1872)

In desperation, the party scattered in search of water, "frequently led astray by the deceptive glimmer of the mirage, or false ponds…those treacherous oases of the desert." They survived only because they found a buffalo "with a stomach distended with water." It had just come from the Cimarron River, (the party did not know that the river was nearby). Gregg continues:

> The hapless intruder [the buffalo] was immediately dispatched [killed], and an invigorating draught [drink] procured from its stomach. I have since heard one of the parties of that expedition declare, that nothing ever passed his lips which gave him such exquisite delight as his first draught of that filthy beverage.

The Growth of Chihuahua. In spite of the dangers, trade was so brisk that by 1824 some Missouri traders found Santa Fe short of money for buying goods. Their economy had been drained by the Spanish, so the people of that small town had little of value to trade. To the south, however, lay Chihuahua, a much larger city and the center of northern Mexico. Perhaps more important, it was a mining town with its own mint for producing coins.

Many of the Missouri goods were soon traded in Chihuahua. Some were brought there directly by Missouri traders who extended their trips down the Chihuahua Trail. Other goods arrived in Chihuahua indirectly. In the early days, most traders from the east were anxious to return home so that they could pay off the bank loans that had supplied their trading money. They sold their goods to New Mexican traders, who in turn sold them in Chihuahua. Prices were only one-third the inflated cost of goods available through Vera Cruz and Mexico City. Missouri goods soon won the northern Mexican market. Some New Mexican traders even began to buy goods at the source; one caravan returning to Missouri in 1825 bought with it two Mexican traders.

A New Road Is Demanded. The Americans were quick to see opportunity. In the spring of 1825, the United States Congress passed a bill sponsored by Missouri's Senator Thomas Hart Benton. It called for funds to lay out a road between Missouri and Santa Fe and to negotiate with the Native Americans for safe passage for caravans along the route. In the next year, a commission surveyed and marked a 750-mile road from Missouri to Taos. The commission's activity had little effect, though, for the western traders made their own routes.

Traveling the Santa Fe Trail

Actually, there was no single Santa Fe Trail. Instead, many tracks crossed the flat, almost bare prairies, then called the "Great American Desert." Without landmarks, and with little water, many traders followed one of the many east- flowing rivers on their way from Missouri to Santa Fe, but certain general routes did become popular.

New Towns Grow up on the Santa Fe Trail. For travelers going west, the Santa Fe Trail began just west of the Mississippi River. Travelers from the northeast often used the Ohio River as the first step of their trip west. At St. Louis, they changed from boats to wagons and pack trains and began their trip across the dry prairie. As a result, St. Louis became an early center for buying supplies to outfit caravans. As western travel grew, other outfitting towns and trading posts developed along the eastern part of the Missouri and

Kansas rivers. Among them were Franklin, Independence, and, later, Westport and Kansas City.

Council Grove. In the early days of the Santa Fe trade, large trading caravans usually started out from the area near Independence, Missouri. Smaller parties often gathered about 150 miles farther along the route at Council Grove. They waited there until they had formed a large enough group for safe crossing. Council Grove consisted of a stand of timber on a small creek, and Josiah Gregg, chronicler of the early Santa Fe trade, warned in 1831:

> Lest this imposing title [Council Grove] suggest to the reader a snug and thriving village, it should be observed, that on the day of our departure from Independence, we passed the last human abode upon our route; therefore, from the borders of Missouri to those of New Mexico not even an Indian settlement greeted our eyes.

The Organization of the Caravan. At Council Grove, the caravan would select its captain and organize itself for travel. The caravan was usually made up of four divisions. Each division chose a lieutenant. The lieutenants formed an advance party, which went ahead of the caravan and scouted the route. They chose the best crossings and prepared the way for the caravan. They cut brush and dug ramps into the steep sides of creeks and ravines. They also marked quicksand areas in the fords with sticks to prevent danger and sometimes made rough bridges of willow branches, grasses, and earth.

Landmarks on the Trail. Once underway, the caravan crossed the headwaters of several streams and rivers, from the south side of the Kansas River to the great bend of the Arkansas River. One of the few outstanding landmarks on the sparce prairie crossing was Pawnee Rock, on which many early travelers carved their names.

Once past the Arkansas River's great bend, travelers could use a variety of crossing points. The clearest and earliest route went along the north side of the Arkansas to the Purgatory (Purgatoire) River. From there, the trail led south through the Raton Pass. This was a hard, steep route. Travelers could also take the Cimarron Cutoff blazed by Becknell. In this case, they forded the Arkansas River just past the great bend and struck out southwest across the desert.

A Permanent Santa Fe Trail Is Cut. In the early years, wise travelers hired experienced guides, for the prairie had many tracks.

Although there was no marked human-made trail, buffalo paths crisscrossed the desert and inexperienced travelers could easily lose their way. As Josiah Gregg described it, these buffalo paths had "...all the appearance of immense highways, over which entire armies would seem to have frequently passed." In 1824, a permanent Santa Fe Trail was cut across the desert. During the spring rains that year, the large annual caravan crossed the prairie. The wagons cut ruts into the already soft ground of the prairie, and these ruts were followed for decades after. In fact, those ruts can still be seen today.

When travelers on the Cimarron Cutoff crossed the desert, broken hills and some springs showed them they were approaching the Rockies. Several landmarks also came into view. Among them were the twin towers of rock called Rabbit Ears and a rocky dome called Round Mound, which travelers often climbed for a view of the countryside. There was also a rock formation, or outcropping, called Point of Rocks. After crossing the headwaters of the Canadian River, the Cimarron Cutoff rejoined the Raton Pass Route and turned south toward Santa Fe.

Travelers sometimes detoured to the top of Round Mound to view the caravan heading toward Santa Fe. (From Josiah Gregg, *Commerce of the Prairies,* 1844)

The Taos Trail and Other Southerly Routes. Another route to Santa Fe, the Taos Trail, was open only to pack trains, in which long lines of mules hauled cargo on their backs. Wagons could not manage the landscape on this route. The route followed the Arkansas River past the Raton Pass turnoff. It then went on into the Sangre de Cristo Mountains to Taos, and then south to Santa Fe.

Other travelers followed more southerly routes west from the Mississippi, such as the Arkansas Route. This route started in Memphis, Tennessee, and ran directly west. Then it met and followed the Arkansas River. At Fort Smith, it reached the frontier. Soon after Fort Smith, the Canadian River split off from the Arkansas. The route then followed the Canadian River much of the way to Santa Fe. The Arkansas Route was a shorter and more direct way to Santa Fe from the Mississippi, but it was used only for late autumn starts, because it lacked a major supply center like St. Louis.

ARRIVING IN SANTA FE

After two decades of the Santa Fe trade, the city still looked to some eyes like "brick-kilns scattered among cornfields." (From W. H. Emory, *Notes of a Military Reconnaissance,* 1846-7)

As caravans approached Santa Fe, they were often encouraged by the arrival of runners, who greeted them as much as 200 miles from the town. These runners, called *avant-couriers*, traveled at night for safety. They arranged for provisions for the Missouri traders. More important, when the runners returned to Santa Fe, they repre-

sented the caravans. They found storage space and arranged customs inspections with the New Mexican authorities.

The State of the Town. Santa Fe itself was a surprise. Josiah Gregg thought he saw "brick-kilns scattered in every direction" in the midst of cornfields. He was surprised to find that he was looking, not at the outskirts, but at the city itself.

The traders, on arrival, went to the buildings around the public square. That was where the government, the guards, and the clergy were housed. Here they negotiated duties, or taxes, with the customshouse officials, who often took a large part of the fees for themselves personally.

By traveling to Santa Fe, the Missouri traders came to the place where the routes from the east and north joined the much older Chihuahua Trail. Santa Fe was the connection between two young nations—Mexico and the United States.

LIFE ON THE TRAIL

The Chihuahua Trail had been in use for well over a century when the Americans arrived. Still, neither trail was a road in the modern sense. The traveling conditions were crude and primitive on both. Where the route was not fixed by a key pass or ford, caravans often

The arrival of a caravan in Santa Fe was an occasion for great rejoicing, when travelers often shot their guns into the air in celebration. (Engraving by A. L. Dick, after drawing by E. Didier, from Josiah Gregg, *Commerce of the Prairies*, 1844)

spread out on the plains. This had positive side effects. Livestock could find fresh grazing and travelers did not have to eat someone else's dust or, worse, get stuck in someone else's mud. No public inns existed along the route. Traders and teamsters alike camped out in the open, even after arriving in one of the many towns. Only a lucky few were invited to stay with well-to-do town families. In the early 1800s, travel was still a great event. When a trading caravan came to town, it was announced by a town crier and often celebrated with a lively ball called a *fandango.*

River Crossings. It was often necessary for the trails to cross rivers, but there were no real bridges or ferries. In high water periods, caravans had to find the best ford, or crossing place, and ride through the water. In extreme cases, they had to float the wagons across on makeshift rafts. After such a crossing, goods had to be spread out on the far side to dry, and then repacked before the traders could move on. In times of low water, caravans sometimes traveled on, or crisscrossed over, dry riverbeds, but the lack of water meant they had to detour off the main route to find fresh water. In either case, travel was hard on the wagons.

Conestoga Wagons. Some traders used simple carts with thick wooden wheels, similar to those used by many Mexicans. Many Missouri traders, however, used Conestoga wagons. These were the well-known canvas-hooded "prairie schooners," often seen in illustrations of pioneers going west. On the high, dry southwestern plateaus, the heat caused wagon wheels to shrink. When this happened, the iron tires had to be refitted to the smaller wheel, and sometimes tied on with rawhide. On the other hand, getting soaked in water made the wood swell and stick. Wagoneers were well-supplied with lubricants such as resin and tallow to make movement easier and cut down on the squeaking of wood on wood. Extra wood for repairs was carried slung under the wagon body, for there was no usable wood along the desert route.

Beasts of Burden. The wagons themselves were usually pulled by oxen or mules. Horses were sometimes used, but they could not compare with oxen and mules for pulling heavy loads. Some travelers and traders rode horses on the trail, and horses were used by the Native Americans of the Plains as well.

The Pack Train. Wagons could easily break down, and could not be used on some routes, such as the Taos Trail, so the pack train was another standard type of caravan on the Chihuahua and Santa Fe trails. A pack train consisted of mules traveling in trains of 50 to 200 animals. They fed on prairie grass and carried as much as 400 pounds each. Pack trains were a cheap alternative to wagon freighting. *Arrieros*, or muleteers, each handling eight or nine animals, were highly respected men on the trail.

Trouble on the Trail. Travel on the Santa Fe and Chihuahua trails was by no means easy—nor was it safe. The Native Americans of the high plains and plateaus did not welcome the invasion into their territory. In the early years of the Santa Fe trade, the Native Americans were more of a potential threat to the caravans rather than an actual danger. Usually they accepted an exchange of goods and livestock and allowed the armed traders to pass unharmed. Traders alone or in small parties were in more danger, though. In 1828, two advance scouts of a caravan were killed, and violence on both sides grew quickly. This made traders more careful about protection on the trails.

The Kansas River area was fairly safe, but wagons still rode in a double column, so that they could easily form a defensive circle if necessary. Once caravans passed Pawnee Rock and moved into Pawnee and Comanche territory, they usually traveled four abreast. Mounted on horses, the Native Americans formed an excellent and formidable light cavalry. As time wore on, they gradually armed themselves with guns—bought or stolen—and became a greater danger to wagon trains.

Escorts for the Caravans. Traders asked for and got U.S. Army escorts, but the inexperienced infantry that was sent at first was no match for the danger. In any case, protection could be supplied only up to the end of American territory, just past Pawnee Rock, where the greatest danger began. The Mexican government sent escorts out from Santa Fe to meet major caravans, but they also did not go into the most dangerous area. Their main job was to catch smugglers who might try to avoid paying customs duties at Santa Fe.

Between the somewhat protected areas on either end of the Santa Fe Trail, travelers had to rely on themselves. They were especially at risk on the Cimarron Cutoff, far from the aid of anyone. The Raton Pass route, which added 100 miles to the trip, turned out to be safer for travelers. Hunters and trappers lived in the area, and had been in the region for decades. These "mountain men" came to the aid of trading caravans. At first they did so unofficially. Later they were paid, and proved to be an effective, armed escort. The most famous of these groups were the Carson men, led by Kit Carson. They guarded many caravans along the Santa Fe Trail.

Bent, St. Vrain & Company. Some of these men even left their mountains and joined in the Santa Fe trade. Most notable among them was a trio of Americans from St. Louis: William and Charles Bent, sons of a judge, and Céran St. Vrain, from a French fur-trading

Many of the mountain routes had been used first by Native Americans and then by mountain men like this one, long before Santa Fe traders came on the scene. (Huntington Library)

family. They formed an organization called Bent, St. Vrain & Company and built a trading fortress on the north side of the Arkansas River, near the junction of the Raton Pass route and the Taos Trail. At the same time, they widened the Raton Pass route to provide easier passage for wagon caravans. It soon became the preferred route for all but the largest, best-protected caravans. These still took the risk of the Cimarron crossing.

Bandits Threaten the Trail.   Between Santa Fe and Chihuahua, the trail was not much safer. The Native Americans there were far from subdued by the Spanish-Americans. In addition to that threat was the danger from bandits, who waited to ambush traders. They knew just when and where to wait. Traders needed travel permits for the trip between Santa Fe and Chihuahua. The permits listed the contents and schedules of the caravans. By paying a small bribe, bandits could get this information from the customs officials, and the risk grew greater.

Travel became even harder when, in 1836, Texas broke away from the Republic of Mexico. Mexico felt that the United States had supported the Texas fight for independence and planned to help New Mexico do the same. So Mexico offered even less protection to the American traders and raised taxes on trade. Texans began to attack New Mexican traders, as well as any Americans who happened to be with them.

Native Americans Increase Attacks along the Trail.   Seeing these attacks on Mexico, and also the unrest throughout the region, the Native American tribes in northern Mexico became far more hostile. They attacked all along the Chihuahua Trail. Many of the smaller villages between Santa Fe and Chihuahua were abandoned at this time. Their people moved to larger towns with better protection.

Trade Flourishes.   In spite of these troubles, trading increased. It is estimated that $15,000 worth of trade took place in 1822. By 1846, the amount had grown to about $1 million. Missouri traders considered Chihuahua to be their main destination. Santa Fe was merely a customs point and city of entry into Mexico. Once in Chihuahua, traders would rent a shop or market stall from which to sell their goods. The most successful traders later rented permanent space. Some, like Céran St. Vrain, even took Mexican citizenship and married into local families.

The Mexicans were so desperate for goods that traders sometimes sold the whole train—teams and wagons and all. Conestoga wagons were highly prized in Mexico, even battered and worn after a 1,300- to 1,400-mile trip. Having traded their goods and wagons for silver, traders sometimes continued on down El Camino Real to Mexico City and Vera Cruz. There they took ships back across the Gulf of Mexico to the Mississippi River and home. Others traded some of their cash for Mexican mules. These, even after a hard drive across the Plains, could be sold for a handsome price in Missouri and Illinois. The rest of the traders made their way back to Missouri in much lighter, smaller, faster caravans.

The silver these Missouri traders brought back with them had a great impact on the Midwestern economy. By 1828, the Mexican peso was more common in the Midwest than the American silver dollar, which had slightly less silver content. By 1831, the peso was the main currency not only in Missouri but in most other Western states. Because of this, these states were not as badly hit as other areas by the economic depression that blighted the rest of the United States in 1837.

THE MEXICAN-AMERICAN WAR

The heyday of the Santa Fe-Chihuahua Trail was brief. Once Chihuahua became the main city on the route, traders wanted to avoid paying duties at Santa Fe. (Duties had to be paid at each city the caravan passed through.) Traders then took new, more direct paths through Texas to Chihuahua, and trade was drained away from the old route.

The United States Takes Control of Santa Fe. Mexico and the United States went to war in 1846. During the course of the war, the United States cavalry moved down the Santa Fe Trail and took Santa Fe without bloodshed. With the area under United States control, traders poured into Santa Fe. They flooded the market, which did not have enough silver to pay for the goods.

The traders then tried to move south to Chihuahua, but their advance party was arrested at El Paso. The rest of their large caravan was stranded for several months in a camp just north of the Journada del Muerto. The traders faced starvation with the coming of winter and bankruptcy because they could not sell their goods. They asked for U.S. Army support and—after some delay—got it.

The United States Takes Control of Chihuahua. On Christmas Day in 1846, United States troops met a Mexican force over twice its size at Rancho del Bracito. After a brief skirmish, the Mexican force retreated down the Chihuahua Trail, followed by United States troops and traders. Some traders bypassed the armies and headed for Chihuahua. But the rest—traders and teamsters handling over 300 wagons—were forced into army service. Early in 1847, at Sacramento, 20 miles north of Chihuahua, U.S. troops defeated the Mexican forces and then moved into occupy Chihuahua. Susan Shelby Magoffin, who had lost her baby on the trail at Bent's Fort, arrived with her trader-husband shortly after Chihuahua was taken over and described the scene:

> ...the good citizens of Chihuahua had never dreamed I dare say that their loved homes would be turned into quarters for common soldiers, their fine houses many of them turned into stables, the rooves made kitchens of, their public *pila* [drinking fountain] used as a bathing trough, the fine trees of their beautiful *almador* [public walk] barked and forever spoiled...

For the next two months, the northern traders desperately tried to unload their goods. When the U.S. Army returned to El Paso, most traders returned with them, except those who had chosen to make Mexico their permanent home.

The Trails During the War. Traders and settlers along the old Chihuahua and Santa Fe trails played important roles in this period—and had hard choices to make about their loyalties and personal interest in events. Certainly, the New Mexicans felt strong ties to the United States traders who had brought them more money and better security. Even Mexico itself had strong ties to the traders. The caravans, with their expert guards, had made the Chihuahua Trail safer than ever before, and had even been trusted to carry the Mexican government's mail and payroll. Even the governor of the territory of New Mexico, now under control, was a trader: Charles Bent, of Bent, St. Vrain & Company. The war with Mexico went on until 1848, and Chihuahua was occupied again, but only temporarily. There was some discussion as to whether or not the whole territory should become part of Texas; but finally, in 1850, the territory of New Mexico became the state of New Mexico, with Santa Fe as its capital.

After the war, the Santa Fe and Chihuahua trails never achieved the significance they had once had. Trade with Mexico continued, but it now followed many routes. Most entered Mexico from El Paso, which was the westernmost point in the state of Texas. (The part of the city on the Mexican side of the border was called Ciudad Juarez, or Juarez City.)

The Era of the Old West. Perhaps more important, the attention of the United States had turned further westward. Tales of western traders, mountain men, and California gold were heard back in the eastern United States. Drawn by these stories, people crossed the Mississippi by the thousands and created that unique and very brief experience known as "The Old West." Along the Santa Fe Trail, Kansas City became the main starting point. Dodge City grew up where the Raton Pass route and the Cimarron Cutoff split. Along the Chihuahua Trail, cowboys bragged of being the "fastest gun west of the Pecos," which was the river running southeast from Santa Fe toward the Gulf of Mexico.

On the Cimarron Cutoff, travelers were often attacked by Native Americans, who resented the intruders. (Indian Alarm on the Cimarron River, from Josiah Gregg, Commerce of the Prairies, Vol. II)

The Oregon-California Trial. The Santa Fe Trail played only a small part in the movement west. Prospectors and settlers heading for California and Oregon usually took the northern overland route known as the Oregon-California Trail. Settlers heading for the

Southwest sometimes followed the old Santa Fe and Chihuahua trails south past Albuquerque, and then west on the Gila Trail, partly along the Gila River Valley. Most travelers to the southwest, however, favored a more southerly route, running through San Antonio and El Paso toward southern California.

Dangers on the Routes. Travel on all of these routes was risky. Bandits, as usual, posed a threat. Native Americans and Mexicans protested for decades against the United States taking the New Mexico territory. Sometimes these protests erupted into violence, bringing danger to travelers and settlers alike. To protect traders and travelers in the western territory, the United States cavalry established a series of armed forts. On the old Santa Fe Trail, Fort Union was built at the point where the Raton Pass route and the Cimarron Cutoff met going west. A new Bent's Fort was built downstream from the site of the original, which had been blown up by William Bent in 1849. Traders soon found that they could profit by supplying the forts with goods, rather than trading down the long trail to Santa Fe and Chihuahua. Some settled down in the towns that grew up along the route, making and selling goods to soldiers and other new settlers.

Stagecoach and Railroad

As traffic going west increased, stagecoach lines came to the old Santa Fe and Chihuahua Trails. However, the main southern stage and mail route ran far to the south of Santa Fe. The Butterfield Southern Overland Mail Route—also called the Oxbow Route—ran 2,800 miles, from St. Louis to San Francisco. From St. Louis, it ran south to Fort Smith, Arkansas, and then southwest through Oklahoma and Texas all the way to El Paso. From there, it went west through Tucson to Yuma, Arizona, and then turned north through California to Los Angeles and San Francisco. Service on the Butterfield Overland Mail line began in 1858 but was cut off at the beginning of the Civil War, in 1861. Four years after the war, in 1869, the transcontinental railroad was completed. By then most long-distance mail was shipped by rail, and the end of the stagecoach lines that had crisscrossed the West was in sight.

The Decline of Santa Fe. Without Chihuahua as its main trading partner, Santa Fe—the oldest colonial settlement in the area—

gradually lost is unique position. In the 1850s and 1860s, when railroads were being planned for the Southwest, Santa Fe was still important enough to be in the plans as the western end of the Atchison, Topeka, and Santa Fe Railroad. During the building of this railroad, the owners even had to fight another railroad for the route through the Raton Pass, which had room for only one railroad.

Trade along the Santa Fe Trail had peaked because of the many new settlers and traders traveling west. In the decades following the Civil War, however, trade dropped sharply. By 1879, the railroad changed its plans, and Santa Fe was bypassed, even though the railroad bore its name. The board of directors thought it would not be worthwhile to swing the line 30 miles north to pass through the city. Instead, the railroad went on west across New Mexico. However, a link to Santa Fe was built in 1880.

THE CATTLE TRAILS

The Era of the Cowboys. The growth of the railroads opened up a brief, colorful period in the history of the American West. Just after the Civil War, the transcontinental railroad began to move west. This made it possible for Texas ranchers to drive their cattle north to the railroad and then sell their stock to buyers who would ship them east by rail. The need for the cattle drive gave birth to the great age of the American cowboy. Small railroad towns like Abilene and Dodge City—and their lawmen and outlaws—became famous in song and story.

The Chisholm Trail. The greatest of all the cattle trails was the Chisholm Trail. It was named after the Scotch-Cherokee trader, Jesse Chisholm. In 1865, Chisholm opened up the northern part of the trail, which ran through what was then Indian Territory. It was used by a few small Texas herds during the next two years but began to be used heavily in late 1867. That year, 35,000-40,000 head of cattle were driven along the Chisholm Trail. After that, ranchers used the trail to drive hundreds of thousands of cattle every year.

The Chisholm Trail started at Laredo, Texas, on the Mexican border, with cattle brought north from Mexico. From there it passed through all of Texas, going north through San Antonio, Austin, Waco, Dallas, and Fort Worth before entering the Indian Territory. Once in Kansas, the trail went through Wichita and then met the Kansas Pacific Railroad at Abilene. Cattle drives from all over Texas joined the trail over a network of many smaller trails and then went north.

Part of the way, as far as Waco, the Chisholm Trail followed the route of the older Shawnee Trail, which had taken cattle directly to St. Louis, on the Mississippi River. In the late 1860s, the Shawnee Trail could no longer be used, because farmers had fenced in much of the land on the way. Farmers objected to the cattle passing over their land, partly because the cattle carried a kind of tick fever, which did not harm the cattle, but killed many other farm animals.

The Western Cattle Trail. Starting in the mid-1870s, some Texas cattle drives began to take a more westerly route, due north out of San Antonio through Fort Griffin and north to Dodge City. This was the Western Cattle Trail, which from then on competed with the Chisholm Trail for Texas cattle. Some Texas herds went on farther north on this trail, to Ogallala, Nebraska, where they met the Union Pacific Railroad.

The Goodnight-Loving Cattle Trail. A much smaller number of Texans drove their cattle west and then north. They took the Goodnight-Loving Cattle Trail. Oliver Loving and Charles Goodnight had pioneered this trail west to the Rockies in 1866. Starting in west Texas, they drove their cattle 700 miles, west across the Pecos River and then north to Fort Sumner, in eastern New Mexico. There they sold part of their herd, and took the rest north for sale in Denver, Colorado. Some later cattle drivers on this trail went farther west, to Albuquerque and Santa Fe.

Great Figures of the Wild West. This was the West of legendary figures such as William "Buffalo Bill" Matthewson, who took a wagon trail north on the Chisholm Trail in the summer of 1867. James B. ("Wild Bill") Hickok was marshall of Abilene in 1871. There were lawmen such as Wyatt Earp and William Barclay ("Bat") Masterston—and outlaws like Sam Bass and John Wesley Harding. These are just some of the names that have become part of United States history and legend.

The days of the great cattle trails lasted just a dozen years or so, starting when the railroads reached the West and ending when a whole network of railroads was built south into Texas. Once the railroads reached the ranchers, there was no longer a need to drive cattle north, and the days of the great cattle trails—and of the heroic trail-town marshals and lawmen—was done.

With the completion of the railroad, the old Santa Fe trade—merchant caravans of prairie schooners pushing across dry, dangerous deserts—came abruptly to an end. The Texas routes to Chihuahua were also soon replaced by railroads. In 1882, the Mexican government completed a railroad along the old Chihuahua Trail, up to El Paso. The Atchison, Topeka, and Santa Fe Railroad built a connecting line to it.

Mexicans challenged the United States border several times in the late 19th and early 20th centuries. They tried it once during the American Civil War, again at the turn of the century, and once again in 1916, before finally accepting the current boundaries. In the same period, the Indian Wars reached their conclusion, and the remaining Native Americans in the area were either deported or forced onto reservations. In these same decades, the ranchers who first opened the lands of the "Great American Desert" to the cattle herds and cowboys were gradually replaced in many areas by farmers. They turned the seeming desert into fertile cropland.

The Trails Today. Although they are no longer of key importance, remains of the Santa Fe and Chihuahua trails still link Mexico and the central prairies of the United States. The Mexican Central Railroad (Ferrocarril Nacional) roughly follows the old route from Chihuahua to Ciudad Juarez, opposite El Paso, Texas. So does Camino [Highway] 45, the old Camino Real from Mexico City to the Rio Grande. U.S. Route 25 takes the route north to Santa Fe and on through the Raton Pass. There at Trinidad, Colorado, a lesser route

Ruts on the Santa Fe Trail, like these just west of Dodge City, Kansas, were cut so deep they can still be seen in some places. (Kansas State Historical Society, Topeka)

swings northwest along the old trail to La Junta, near the site of Bent's Fort. The trail is completed by U.S. Route 50, which follows the Arkansas River through Dodge City to Kansas City. That city's size and importance owe a large debt to the Santa Fe and Chihuahua trails. U.S. Route 56 from Dodge City across to Springer, New Mexico, roughly follows the old Cimarron Cutoff.

In all of these routes, modern engineering and nature's changes have caused shifts in the roadbed from one side of a riverbank to the other, or through the now-more-stable Médanos sand dunes, rather than around them. But the main course of the Santa Fe and Chihuahua trails remains the same—trails which have played such a large role in the history of the United States and Mexico. As historical geographer Ellen Churchill Semple put it:

> ...every wagon-track and mule-trail across the plains marked the passing of the shuttle weaving northern Mexico and the American Republic into one fabric.

SUGGESTIONS FOR FURTHER READING

Cleland, Robert Glass. *This Reckless Breed of Men: The Trappers and Fur Traders of the Southwest* (New York: Knopf, 1963). Focuses on activities on the mountain trails.

Connor, Seymour V. and Jimmy M. Skaggs. *Broadcloth and Britches: The Santa Fe Trade* (College Station and London: Texas A & M University Press, 1977). A detailed, lively account of the trade between Santa Fe and Missouri.

Gard, Wayne. *The Chisholm Trail* (Norman, Oklahoma: University of Oklahoma Press, 1954). A sound history of the Chisholm, Loving-Goodnight, Western, and other cattle trails, which includes many colorful stories.

Garrard, Lewis H. *Wah-To-Yah and the Taos Trail*, ed. by Ralph B. Bieber (Glendald, California: Arthur H. Clark Company, 1938). A firsthand account of a young tourist traveling with Céran St. Vrain's caravan in 1846–47.

Gregg, Josiah. *Commerce of the Prairies*, ed. by Max L. Moorhead (Norman, Oklahoma: University of Oklahoma Press, 1954; reprint of a 19th-century edition). A classic account of the Santa Fe-Chihuahua trade by one of the main traders along the route.

Magoffin, Susan Shelby. *Down the Santa Fe Trail and Into Mexico: The Diary of Susan Shelby Magoffin, 1846-1847*, ed. by Stella M. Drumm (New Haven: Yale University Press, 1926). The

journal of a young bride traveling with her husband, one of the
Magoffin trading family.

Moody, Ralph. *The Old Trails West* (New York: Crowell, 1963). A
brief history of each of the main western trails; includes chapters
on the Oregon and California Trails, with excellent maps.

Moorhead, Max L. *New Mexico's Royal Road: Trade and Travel on
the Chihuahua Trail* (Norman, Oklahoma: University of Oklahoma Press, 1958). A prime history of the route between Chihuahua and Santa Fe.

Perrigo, Lynn I. *Our Spanish Southwest* (Dallas: Banks Upshaw
and Co., 1960). A strong overview with much detail.

Vestal, Stanley. *Old Santa Fe Trail* (Boston: Houghton Mifflin,
1939). An attempt at re-creation; not a history.

5

THE OREGON TRAIL
AND THE CALIFORNIA
TRAIL

Ever since the first Europeans came to the continent of North America, settlers, pioneers, and explorers were drawn westward. In the 50 years after the American Revolution, millions of people poured across the Appalachian Mountains through the Mohawk River Valley or the Cumberland Gap. On the way, they claimed land all the way west to the Mississippi River. Native Americans were pushed out and forced, by treaty, to live on lands farther west. The settlers paused, but not for long. They kept looking west, past the forests and the central prairies and out toward the Rocky Mountains and beyond. To complete this quest, they developed the Oregon Trail and the California Trail.

The Many Attempts at the Push West. In a way, the search for these trails was part of the great voyage west that had started with Christopher Columbus. Seafaring peoples of Western Europe first came to the Americas in the 15th and 16th centuries when seeking the Indies and China. The English and French in America searched for 300 years for a Northwest Passage, a northern route through to the Pacific Ocean. Explorers such as Champlain, La Salle, Joliet, and Marquette went west on the St. Lawrence River, through the Great Lakes to the Mississippi, exploring the huge American heartland and searching for a passage to the Pacific. The Lewis and Clark expedition, in the early 1800s, showed the desire of the young nation of the United States to continue the push west.

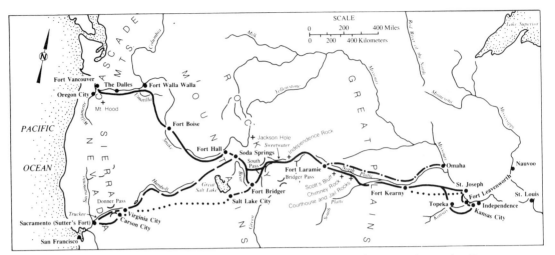

The Oregon Trail and the California Trail in the Mid-19th Century

——————— Oregon Trail

— — — — California Trail

—·—·— Mormon Trail

········ Pony Express Route

The Nature of the Trails. Beginning in the 1840s, the Oregon and California trails were the routes to the westernmost lands of the continent. It was a long, hard trip—a thousand mile walk over prairie and high plains, followed by another thousand miles of mountain, desert, and white-water river country. Despite its harshness, in just a few decades, over a quarter of a million people went west on the Oregon and California trails. These included farmers and ranchers looking for a place to settle, traders and trappers, groups of people suffering from religious persecution, and gold-seekers hoping to get rich quickly. Almost all of those who took the trails to Oregon and California made it. As a result, they completed the long journey across the North American continent that had started at Plymouth Rock and Jamestown over 200 years before.

EARLY TIMES IN THE OREGON COUNTRY

Other Names for the Route. The migration of large numbers of people to the Oregon country did not get under way until the 1840s. When it did, the several routes the migrants used became known together as the Oregon and California trails. The trails have also been called the Oregon Trace, The Emigrant Road, and the Great

Platte Trail. Some parts of the route have also been called the Overland Trail, the California Overland Trail, and the Mormon Trail. Much of the trail from the Missouri River out to the Oregon ran closely beside a great Native American trail called the Big Medicine Trail. Francis Parkman, an American historian who lived in the 1800s, first called the route the Oregon Trail, and this is the name by which it is best known.

Most of those who traveled the trail went to California, rather than to Oregon and the northwest. However, before 1846, the entire area west of the Rocky Mountains and north of California was called Oregon, in contrast to the smaller area known by that name today. So emigrants who were traveling to California went through hundreds of miles of the Oregon country before branching off on the California Trail.

The Missouri River. Even before the large migration began in the 1840s, there was activity in the Oregon country. Much of this activity had the Missouri River as its common starting point. Water from much of the northeastern slope of the American Rockies drains into the Missouri. Then it flows east through Montana and southwest through the Dakotas, Nebraska, and Kansas. There it turns east again, crosses Missouri and joins the Mississippi River at St. Louis. The towns along the bend in the river on the Kansas-Missouri border were often starting places for early explorers searching for a route to the Oregon country, as well as for those who followed their trails later.

THE LEWIS AND CLARK ROUTE

In 1792, Thomas Jefferson proposed a northwest expedition. He thought it could go by way of the Missouri and Columbia rivers. The journey did not start right away, but Jefferson's interest in the northwest eventually led to the Lewis and Clark expedition which began during Jefferson's term as president of the United States. Meriwether Lewis and George Rogers Clark started up the Missouri on May 14, 1804, a little over two months after the United States purchased the Louisiana Territory from France. Lewis and Clark found the main water route west. They went north and then west on the Missouri and crossed over the Continental Divide in what is now northern Montana. The Continental Divide is the crest of the Rocky Mountains, the line that divides waters that flow to the

In narrow valleys, westbound travelers often had to crisscross from side to side to find a trail fit for wagons. (National Archives)

Pacific from those that flow to the Atlantic. The explorers found their way into the Columbia River system—first the Snake River, which took them to the Columbia itself and then down to the sea. This was, for the Americans, the real opening of the Northwest. It was their Northwest Passage to the Pacific and pointed the way toward the Oregon Trail that came later.

Political Power on the Oregon Trail. The Oregon Trail did not follow the Lewis and Clark route. This was partly a matter of distance—the Lewis and Clark route was not very direct. It was also, however, a matter of the power of Native American groups. From the 1820s through the early years of the Oregon-California migration, the powerful Blackfoot Confederation blocked the upper Missouri route. The route that later became the Oregon Trail, on the other hand, had no strong Native American opposition. The United States could not use the army to clear the way until 1846. Between 1818 and 1846, the Oregon country was claimed by both Great Britain and the United States. It was controlled by a very uneasy agreement between the two nations. After 1846, the Oregon territory was divided up between Great Britain and the United States. At that point, the Missouri-Columbia river route might have been opened for emigrants to Oregon, but by then the main routes west were well set, and the way west was the Oregon Trail.

The Political State of California. California, too, was not really open to Americans before 1846. A few Americans had come by sea or overland through the Southwest in earlier years, and a few hundred more had reached California in the early 1840s. California and the rest of the huge area from west Texas to the Pacific and from Oregon to the Rio Grande were part of Mexico. California was not part of the United States until it was won during the United States–Mexican War of 1846–48.

MOUNTAIN MEN

After the Lewis and Clark expedition, American trappers and traders began to explore the country between the Missouri and the Pacific. They moved into the Jackson Hole and Yellowstone country and built a fort at the mouth of the Big Horn River. In 1811, John Jacob Astor's Pacific Fur Company sent an overland party from the Missouri to the mouth of the Columbia. They built Fort Astoria there but because of wartime pressure were forced to sell it in 1813 to the British Northwest Company. During the next decade, there was much independent trapping and trading along the upper Missouri.

The Rocky Mountain Fur Company. Then, in the 1820s, the Rocky Mountain Fur Company was formed. Now American trappers moved out from the Missouri River into the West. They took large amounts of furs, competing with the Northwest Company and later with Astor's new American Fur Company. In the process, they traveled the old Native American trails up the Platte River and out through the western mountains. Among these trappers and traders were Jim Bridger, Kit Carson, William Sublette, and Tom

Fitzpatrick. They were the early trailblazers and guides along the Oregon, California, and Mormon trails.

The Emigrant Parties

The first two groups of emigrants to the Oregon country were led by Nathaniel Wyeth in 1832 and 1833. They were pioneers in settling the general route of the Oregon Trail. Their path went northwest up the Platte and the Sweetwater rivers, through South Pass to the Snake River, and out to the Columbia and the Willamette Valley. The first party, in 1832, had trapper William Sublette as guide. It went to Pierre's Hole, which was a little to the north of the site where Fort Hall was later built. Then it went south and west to the Snake. Later, it followed an old Native American trail out to Fort Walla Walla on the Columbia.

The second party went through South Pass and south to the new Fort Bridger. Moving northwest again, they built Fort Hall, left some of the party there, and then moved on to Oregon. They also took the old Native American water routes through the mountains. This party followed the shorter Umatilla River into the Columbia, by passing Fort Walla Walla. These were the basic routes that would be used by hundreds of thousands of emigrants west for the next 50 years.

A few other small emigrant parties reached Oregon in the 1830s. They came by both land and sea, and some groups included missionaries. A trickle of Americans also went into Spanish California, using the southern land route and the sea. Even as a result of these emigrant groups, in all, there were probably no more than a few hundred Americans in California by 1840 and perhaps only 500 Americans in Oregon's Willamette Valley. All this was soon to change.

Oregon Fever

These settlers wrote back home about huge new landholdings and the richness and promise of the new land. Their letters were widely publicized throughout the country by newspaper editors, politicians, and clergy. Throughout the 1830s, "Oregon fever," "Oregon societies," and "California societies" began to grow.

The Role of Senator Benton. Another important influence in the push west was Senator Thomas Hart Benton of Missouri, a strong supporter of American westward expansion. For 30 years, from 1821 to 1851, Benton pushed for expansion into the West. His greatest victory was to win federal financing for the western surveying and mapping trip of his son-in-law, John C. Frémont, in 1842. The trip itself had little to do with the mapping of the West. Frémont mainly took quite well-worn and well-known Native American, trapper, and emigrant paths, but it was a huge publicity victory and added to the Oregon fever of the time. Many more emigrants went to Oregon as a result.

In the three years before the Frémont expedition, only a few hundred emigrants went to Oregon and California. But in 1843, after the expedition, almost 1,000 emigrants went all the way from the Missouri to the Willamette. From then on, 1843 was known as the year of the "Great Emigration" to Oregon, and travel to Oregon grew each year afterwards. As a result, the balance of population and power in Oregon changed greatly. The Pacific Northwest was ready for American control, and a treaty with Great Britain in 1846 made this a reality. The great push west had begun.

THE OREGON TRAIL

Every spring, starting in 1841, westbound emigrants gathered at the bend in the Missouri River on the border of Kansas and Missouri. They set off together toward Oregon and California, starting

This ford, at the mouth of Deer Creek, was one of several places where travelers could rather easily cross the Platte River. (*Crossing the Platte, Mouth of Deer Creek*, by F. R. Grist, from Howard Stansbury, *Exploration and Survey of the Valley of the Great Salt Lake*, 1852)

from places such as Kansas City, Liberty, Fort Leavenworth, and St. Joseph. But most gathered at Independence, Missouri, which is considered to be the start of the Oregon Trail.

The Geography of the Trail. Going west out of Independence, travelers were not yet on an Oregon-bound trail. They were on the Santa Fe Trail, which ran from St. Louis to Santa Fe. Nine miles out of Independence, they crossed the Missouri state line into treaty-granted Indian Country (later the state of Kansas). Forty-one miles out, the road branched, and the separate Oregon-California Trail began. In the early days, this was marked by a small hand-lettered sign that read Road to Oregon.

For the next 60 miles, the Oregon Trail went almost due west to the Kansas River. There were ferries at several places along the Kansas, some of them run by displaced Shawnee and Delaware Indians. The main crossing in the later years was the Topeka ferry. Crossing the Kansas River, the emigrants turned northwest. They traveled across the prairie to the South Fork of the Platte River, a distance of a little over 200 miles.

Travelers usually covered this part of the route in the spring. Most of the wagons set out from Independence in May so they could cross the Cascade Mountains, 2,000 miles away, before the snow blocked the mountain passes in the autumn. In the spring, the flowering prairie was fairly easy to cross. The harder parts of the trail were far ahead.

At the Platte River, the Oregon Trail turned west again, following the south bank of the river 450 miles across the Great Plains and into the Rocky Mountains. The trail climbed several thousand feet, but the climb was made over so long a distance that most people did not feel it. Going across the Rockies, the land and climate changed. As the travelers pushed west, forest and river valley gave way to lush grasslands. Along the Platte River, grassland gave way to treeless prairie, and then to the dry scrub and windswept rock of the high plains. As the emigrants followed the Platte River across most of present-day Nebraska and part of Wyoming, they entered the American West.

Buffalo along the Trail. Along the Platte, the travelers began to see and hunt buffalo. Because wood was scarce, they used buffalo dung, or "chips," as their main source of fuel for fires. The herds of buffalo were huge. An early migrant, in 1841, provides this description:

I have seen the plain black with them for several days' journey as far as the eye could reach. They seemed to be coming northward continually from the distant plains to the Platte to get water, and would plunge in and swim across by thousands—so numerous were they that they changed not only the color of the water, but its taste, until it was unfit to drink; but we had to use it.

The Oregon-California Trail followed the south bank of the Platte, and then the south fork of the Platte, for well over 100 miles. The travelers then crossed the South Platte and cut across country to meet the North Platte. They followed it west almost 200 miles more to Fort Laramie. This was high-plains country. The altitude made work and walking much harder, and the land was very harsh.

While following the North Platte, the emigrants saw striking rock formations such as the Courthouse and Jail Rocks. Another, called Chimney Rock, could be seen from many miles away across the plains. Farther on, they found the huge rock formations at Scott's Bluff, which is now an American national monument.

Life on the Trail. In his classic account of the Oregon-bound migration of 1843, Jesse Applegate gave a vivid picture of a typical busy morning on the prairie.

At night, wagon trains formed a circle not only for defense but also to keep livestock like these unbridled horses from straying. (Denver Public Library, Western History Department)

It is four o'clock A.M.; the sentinels on duty have discharged [shot] their rifles—the signal that the hours of sleep are over—and every wagon and tent is pouring forth its night tenants, and slow-kindling smokes begin largely to rise and float away in the morning air. Sixty men start from the corral, spreading as they make through the vast herd of cattle and horses that make a semicircle around the encampment, the most distant perhaps two miles away.

According to Applegate, the herders would then go outside the semicircle of cattle to check for tracks that would indicate whether any animals had strayed or been stolen. After that, it was time to herd the cattle into a smaller circle.

Meanwhile, breakfast was being prepared, the wagons loaded, and the teams yoked. All the preparations done, it was time again for the caravan to move. Applegate gives a vivid picture of a wagon train ready to begin its day's journey:

It is on the stroke of seven; the rush to and fro, the cracking of whips, the loud command to oxen, and what seemed to be the inextricable confusion of the last ten minutes had ceased. Fortunately every one has been found and every teamster is at his post. The clear notes of a trumpet sound in the front; the pilot and his guards mount their horses; the leading divisions of the wagons move out of the encampment, and take up the line of march; the rest fall into their places with the precision of clock work....

The caravan continued west, on to the next encampment. At Fort Laramie, over 600 miles from the Missouri, most emigrant trains rested for a few days. Then they went on northwest along the North Platte. They crossed to its north bank well over 100 miles farther on, near what is now Casper, Wyoming. This was the final crossing of the North Fork of the Platte. It was very difficult until 1847, when Mormon's Ferry was built.

THE MORMAN TRAIL AND FERRY

The Mormon Church formed a major 19th-century Christian sect. The Mormons were persecuted and expelled from several places in the eastern and midwestern United States, and in 1846, were expelled from their center at Nauvoo, Illinois. By the spring of 1847, they were on the Missouri River, north of the Platte River.

That spring, an advance party led by Brigham Young set out west. The party crossed the Missouri and went south to the Platte. They then followed the Platte and the North Platte west and northwest to Laramie. This route was the first portion of the Mormon Trail.

The Trails Merge. At Laramie, the Mormon Trail joined the main route of the Oregon-California Trail. The trails continued together until they reached Fort Bridger. There, the second part of the Mormon Trail split off toward the southwest and ended at the Great Salt Lake, where Salt Lake City, Utah, was established. In all, the Mormon Trail went from Omaha, Nebraska, to Salt Lake City, a distance of over 1,000 miles.

The Institution of the Ferry. When Brigham Young's party crossed the North Platte near Laramie, the river was nearly at flood stage. But the Mormons had brought along a boat, called the *Revenue Cutter*, and used it to ford the river. Other emigrant trains behind the Mormons could not cross the high river without boats or ferries. The Mormons provided both—for a fee. The boat took people and goods, and a ferry they had quickly built on the spot took wagons. Most of the Mormon party continued on, traveling the main trail, but they left behind their ferry and some people to run it. The Mormon Ferry remained intact until the river was bridged two decades later.

Independence Rock, where tens of thousands of emigrants carved their names, has been called the Great Register of the Oregon, California, and Mormon trails. (Wyoming Travel Commission)

After this final crossing of the Platte, the westward trail headed away from the river. It ran across 50 miles of dry country to the Sweetwater River Valley. At this point, travelers had 900 miles of grassland and high plains behind them, and well over 1,000 miles of mountains, deserts, and rivers ahead. Near the beginning of the Sweetwater Valley was Independence Rock, which has been called the Greater Register of the Oregon, California, and Mormon trails. Tens of thousands of emigrants inscribed their names on the huge grey granite rocks, just as many lone trappers had done in earlier years. Then they headed into the Rockies.

The Halfway Point Is Reached. The valley of the Sweetwater ran clear and level for 100 miles, although the surrounding country was very rough. It ran up through South Pass, a 20-mile-wide, easy-to-travel cut through the mountains. The pass is high—almost 7,500 feet above sea level—but the approach to it is so gradual and easy that many emigrants did not know when they had reached the top of the pass and were starting down the other side. At that point, those bound for the Pacific Coast —for Oregon and California—were halfway there. They had entered Oregon country.

Twenty miles west of South Pass, travelers had to make a choice. Most of those bound for California and Oregon took the most direct route west. It was named Sublette's Cutoff, after the fur trader who had first used it. This route went through 110 miles of mostly desert country. It was a long, straight haul across hard, almost waterless country to the Green River.

Smaller groups sometimes took a somewhat longer route. They went Southwest to Fort Bridger, a small trading post founded by mountain man and trapper Jim Bridger and his partner, Louis Vasquez. These groups then turned northwest and rejoined the main trail at the Green River. This route avoided the hardships of Sublette's Cutoff and was a little easier on the animals and people. It was, though, about 80 miles longer.

Mormon emigrants went from Fort Bridger to Salt Lake City. To do so, they struggled over 120 miles of very rough country.

Fort Hall Is Reached. From the Green River, however, most emigrants bound for California and Oregon went along the main trail toward Fort Hall. This was 125 miles farther northwest, up the Bear River, and close to where the trail met the Snake River.

Fort Hall had been built by New Englander Nathaniel Wyeth in 1834, during the days of the fur trade. For those on the Oregon-California Trail, it formed a much-needed resting place. For many, it was also a place to make the final choice between California and Oregon.

The Trails to California and Oregon Divide

Forty miles southwest of Fort Hall, at the Raft River, the trails forked. The trail to Oregon followed the southern bank of the Snake River. The trail to California turned south, along the Raft. This part of the trail had the highest crossing on the California and Oregon trails—the 8,000-foot pass over the divide at the eastern end of the Bear River Valley. Like South Pass, however, it was an easy climb.

Trials for Those on the Oregon Trail. Travelers on the Oregon Trail now faced the hardest part of the journey. Following the valley of the Snake were 300 miles of desert. A very hard climb over the Blue Mountains into Oregon came next. Beyond Fort Boise the trail left the Snake River and followed the Powder River Valley up and over the Blue Mountains. Most early emigrants swung north to Fort Walla Walla, where many stopped to rest. By 1844, most emigrants bypassed Fort Walla Walla; instead, they took a shorter route along the Umatilla River and into the Columbia River.

Then came a slow overland road almost 200 miles down the Columbia River to a settlement called The Dalles. In the early years, that was followed by a very hard final 60 miles by boat or raft down the Columbia itself. Livestock were driven over a narrow mountain trail south of Mount Hood. Emigrants faced a long portage past the Cascade Mountains, 40 miles from Fort Vancouver. By 1846, though, the Barlow Road had been built to avoid the final 60 miles down the river. Emigrants followed this wagon road from The Dalles to Oregon City, in the Willamette Valley. When they reached the Willamette Valley, the emigrants were at the end of the 2,000-mile-long Oregon Trail.

The California Trail. Whereas the Oregon Trail headed northwest, the California Trail ran in a more westerly direction. Immigrants to California had several routes to choose from beyond South

Pass. Some turned west before Fort Hall. They cut across 70 miles of rough country up the Bear River to Soda Springs. From there, they went southwest, toward the Humboldt River and California.

The second choice involved passing through Salt Lake City, which had been founded in 1847. Some travelers took the last section of the Mormon Trail instead of going northwest from Fort Bridger. Taking the Mormon Trail was longer, but emigrants could stop in Salt Lake City to rest and make repairs before crossing the desert and mountains to California.

The main route to California went through Fort Hall and the Raft River. Whichever trail was taken, all three came together again farther west, at the Humboldt River. This was the main way west to California.

The Humboldt River. The main California route followed the Humboldt for over 350 miles. Unlike the route to Oregon along the Snake River, the passage along the Humboldt was easy, with water and grass all the way. Then, the Humboldt actually sank out of sight into the desert and marsh area called the Humboldt Sink. From there, travelers had to cross over 50 miles of very hard, waterless, desert to the Truckee River. The trail followed the Truckee River for 100 miles. It went over the Sierra Nevada mountains and down into the Bear Valley of northern California. This was the end of the trail.

In the snow-covered Sierra Nevada, the survivors from the Donner party were finally rescued by a relief party from California. (Bancroft Library)

The Ill-Fated Donner Emigrant Train. The final approach to California was called the Donner Pass, named after the ill-fated Donner emigrant train of 1846. The Donner party came through the pass late that year and was unable to make it across because of snow. Finally, 47 of the 87 people perished, and some of the living cannibalized the dead in order to survive. It was a high, difficult pass; but most emigrants made it over safely.

The Safer Carson Route Is Opened. After 1848, a second, somewhat easier route across the mountains was found. This was the Carson Route. It was opened that year by a group of Mormons going from California to Salt Lake City. The Carson Route, named after the Carson River, runs about 25 miles south of the Truckee route. It moves west along the Carson River, then over the mountains to Lake Tahoe. From the crest of the Sierra Nevada, coming by either the Truckee or Carson routes, it is less than 100 miles to the end of the California Trail. That 100 miles is mostly downhill and then across the level Sacramento Valley, to Sutter's Fort, now called Sacramento.

Risks of the Trails

Whether to Sutter's Fort in California or to Fort Vancouver on the Willamette, the routes west were long and arduous—2,000 miles of high plains, mountain range, desert, and mountain range again. The worst mountain pass on each trail was at the western end. Travelers reached these passes exhausted, and a heavy snow blocking the mountain pass could threaten their lives. At best, emigrants could hope to cross the last pass into Oregon or California after three-and-a-half to four months on the trail. They would reach their destination in late August or early September. At worst, parties that started late or had some bad luck might find themselves struggling through the western mountains in late October or even early November.

Modes of Transport on the Trails. The wagons were the main problem. These were generally not the huge horse-drawn Conestoga wagons commonly seen in Western films, which transported the whole family as well as their belongings. Most were oxen-drawn covered farm wagons, with drivers walking alongside. Indeed, most emigrants walked to California, with only some children and the sick riding on the wagons. Wagons were for hauling food, water, and belongings. The more strongly built and lightly loaded the wagon, the better chance it had of getting through. Most emigrants to Oregon, California, and Salt Lake City were successful in getting through, though many had to abandon goods, animals, and vehicles along the way.

In all, well over a quarter of a million people walked west between the early 1840s and the late 1860s. Then the railroads began to take the lion's share of the westbound traffic.

GOLD RUSH DAYS

The emigration to California was small at first, but the discovery of gold at Sutter's Fort changed that, resulting in the California Gold Rush of 1849. In 1848, only about 400 Americans went overland by way of the California Trail. In 1849, the number had risen to about 25,000. In 1850, the number had risen again to about 44,000. By this time, gold fever had taken hold so much that Americans were also entering California in large numbers by sea and by land routes from the south.

Hard Times on the Trails. The years of 1849 and 1850 were terribly hard for most travelers on the California and Oregon trails. Many were gold-seekers, poorly prepared and badly equipped for the 2,000-mile trek to California. Grass along the trails had been used up by the earliest of the tens of thousands of settlers, leaving little to feed the livestock of those who came later. Game was scarce to nonexistent. Many parties ran completely out of water on the desert. The trails themselves were not harder to travel. In fact, they were easier, because good ferries had been created, the first bridge had been built across the Platte, and the trails had been beaten down by thousands of wagons. However, because of the numbers of emigrants and their bad preparation, there was great hardship, and death was commonplace.

The Cholera Epidemic. In 1849, cholera struck the huge emigrant trains pouring west. Cholera is a contagious, often fatal disease of the digestive system. Many emigrants had brought it with them to the gathering points on the Missouri, and it spread from there. F. A. Chenoweth, who traveled in that year, reported that:

Very soon after the assembled throng took up its march over the plains the terrible wave of cholera struck them in a way to carry the utmost terror and dismay into all parts of the moving mass...This terrible malady seemed to spend its most deadly force on the flat prairie...and about Fort Laramie.

Another traveler, backed up at a river crossing in midsummer, saw the danger of having so many people crowded together:

> ...here at this time are two or three hundred wagons with their accompanying teams of men, and the ground is covered with a coat of light dust two inches in depth, which the wind is constantly carrying to and from, whilst the sun is pouring down his hottest rays upon us, and the wonder is that some of us only and not all of us are sick.

Migration Numbers Decline. The California emigration slowed to a trickle in 1851, as stories of hardship and people who had lost everything drifted back east. Even the Oregon migration slowed a little that year, but over 3,500 still made it to Oregon, although only a little over 1,000 went to California.

The flow of emigration, however, was soon to grow. A large steady flow of farmers and storekeepers moved through the high plains and over the western mountains to settle northern California and the Pacific Northwest. In only 11 years, from 1849 through 1860, well over 200,000 people went west overland on the California Trail. Almost 55,000 went to the Willamette Valley on the Oregon Trail; almost 45,000 went to the Salt Lake City area on the Mormon Trail. The total number approached 300,000.

A Steady Flow of Emigrants Travels on the Trails. The American Civil War and the Indian Wars greatly slowed travel west of the Missouri, but only for a few years. By 1865, and every year after that until the railroads began to take most of the traffic, tens of thousands of wagons went west on the Oregon, California, and Mormon trails. By this time, though, many were not going all the way through to the Pacific states. Instead, they were settling and mining the high plains and mountain states. There was no longer just one main trail with three branches going northwest. A network of smaller trails and roads had developed that served the local areas.

The trails themselves changed. Bridges, ferries, toll roads, and many new cutoffs across the mountains into California and Oregon were constructed. At first, federal and local governments had done little to improve these main routes but by the late 1850s had begun building roads and bridges on the trails. By 1853, both the Laramie and the Platte had been bridged. By 1859, the main route across the South Pass had been relocated. The new road was called the Landers Cutoff, after the engineer who had chosen the new route for the federal government.

More Gold Is Discovered. There were new discoveries of gold and silver. In 1859, there was a small gold strike near Denver, which was soon used up, but it precipitated a gold rush that brought many thousands of gold-seekers out along the trail to Colorado. Their slogan, "Pike's Peak or Bust," referred to the striking mountain called Pike's Peak on the edge of the Great Plains. In the same year, a huge gold strike—the Comstock Lode—was made east of the Sierra Nevada, near Lake Tahoe. Thousands of gold-seekers, from both east and west, arrived by using the California Trail. They settled the Carson City–Virginia City area of Nevada.

The Bozeman Trail. Gold-seekers also traveled to the northwest in 1863, when gold was discovered in Montana. Another town called Virginia City grew there, as well as a new trail to the northwest. This was the Bozeman Trail, started by John M. Bozeman in the spring of 1863. It ran from the Platte River near Fort Laramie in Wyoming, northwest to Virginia City, Montana. It followed old Native American trails, and part of its route went along the Platte and Yellowstone rivers. The main freight carriers preferred the Bozeman Trail because it went through easy country. The Bozeman Trail was heavily used, but only for about five years. Then the transcontinental railroad was completed, and most traffic went by rail. By then, too, there were steamboats on the upper Missouri and the Yellowstone, which took much of the traffic that had previously gone by wagon.

Busy Times on the Trails. As the whole region between the Missouri and the Pacific became settled, overland trade and the coast-to-coast mail service grew. By the 1860s, emigrants on the overland trails were joined by thousands of large freight wagons and tens of thousands of oxen. These carried army and civilian goods throughout the West. The largest carrier was called the Central Overland California and Pike's Peak Express Company, and worked out of Leavenworth, Kansas. It ran over 6,000 wagons and 75,000 oxen. It carried freight on the Oregon, California, and Mormon trails, as well as all over the northern mountains and Plains year-round.

The Pony Express. The Pike's Peak Express Company also started the first fast transcontinental mail route—the Pony Express. The Pony Express route ran almost 2,000 miles. It started at St. Joseph, a little east of the Missouri and north of Independence. It ran beside the main line of the Oregon Trail to Fort Kearny. There it joined the main trail and traveled with it all the way up the Platte and the Clearwater to Fort Bridger. From there it took the road to Salt Lake City, and then went south of and beside the Humboldt River section of the California Trail. It went to Carson City, Virginia City, and across the mountains south of Lake Tahoe to Placerville, Sacramento, and San Francisco.

The Pony Express service did not last long. It operated for only about a year and a half, from April 3, 1860, until October 24, 1861, when the first transcontinental telegraph line was completed. Despite its brief history, it has continued to foster the imagination and interest of many people. Such riders as Pony Bob Haslam, who carried copies of Lincoln's Inaugural Address west through storm and ambush, were great popular heroes in their day. The Pony Express provided 10-day mail service to California, and helped hold the West for the Union during the Civil War.

STAGECOACH DAYS

Daily overland stage and mail service from Missouri to California started in July 1861. For the first year, it followed the main Oregon Trail to Fort Bridger, Salt Lake City, and Sacramento. After that, it followed the Oregon Trail only as far as Julesburg, Colorado, on the Platte, about 100 miles west of Fort Kearny. There it joined the Cherokee Trail, also known as the Central Overland Trail.

The Cherokee Trail ran from Fort Smith, Arkansas, to Fort Bridger, and dated from 1849, when a wagon train that included some Cherokees forged this route on the way to California. At Fort

Bridger, it rejoined the California Trail. The stage line ran to Denver, across the mountains to Fort Bridger, then to Salt Lake City, and west to California, following much the same route as the Pony Express.

THE RAILROADS

After the Civil War, the railroads came west and use of the old trails declined. There were still emigrant wagons on the Oregon Trail as late as the 1890s, and freight wagons even later than that, but the railroads were faster, cheaper, and easier to use. Most traffic began to shift to the railroads soon after they were built.

In 1863, the Central Pacific Railroad started building east from California, and in 1865, the Union Pacific Railroad started building west from Omaha. The two lines met on May 10, 1869, and soon replaced the main wagon trails west. Along the Platte and Humboldt, the railroad followed parts of the old Oregon and California trails. The same is true of the Union Pacific line northwest to Walla Walla, and the Oregon short line from Walla Walla to Portland.

Modern Times

Today, the trails are gone, but there are highways that still run along sections of the three trails. U.S. Routes 80 and 26 run along the Platte. Routes 30 and 84 run northwest out across Idaho and Oregon, beside the Snake and the Columbia. Farther south, U.S. Routes 40 and 95 take the old Truckee and Donner Pass route through Reno, Nevada, and over the mountains to Sacramento. U.S. Route 50 takes the more southerly Carson River route through Carson City and Virginia City to the south shore of Lake Tahoe and then to Sacramento.

All the way from the Missouri to the Pacific, and from the Canadian border deep into the American Southwest, there are markers, monuments, museums, and festivals that commemorate the old Oregon, California, and Mormon trails, and all the trails that fed

In some lightly settled parts of the upper Great Plains, you can still see the ruts like these, cut over a century ago by thousands of wagons on the old Oregon Trail. (Wyoming Travel Commission)

them. These were the roads that opened the last American frontier and completed the long-sought voyage west.

Suggestions for Further Reading

Billington, Ray Allen. *The Far Western Frontier, 1830–1860* (New York: Harper and Row, 1962; reprint of the 1956 ed.). A good general history of western frontier of the period, with a chapter on backgrounds and on the Oregon, California, and Mormon trails.

———. *The Westward Movement in the United States* (New York: Van Nostrand Reinhold, 1959). A useful general history of the American westward movement from sea to sea.

Chapman, Arthur. *The Pony Express: The Record of a Romantic Venture in Business* (New York: Cooper Square, 1971). A popular history of the Pony Express.

Drago, Harry Sinclair. *Roads to Empire: The Dramatic Conquest of the American West* (New York: Dodd Mead, 1968). A brief history of most of the main American western trails, with a detailed treatment of Mormon Trail.

Federal Writers' Project, *Oregon Trail* (New York: Hastings House, 1939). A brief history and traveler's guide, with much detail of sites along the old trail.

Ghent, W. J. *Road to Oregon* (New York: Longmans, 1929). A full treatment of the Oregon, California, and Mormon trails.

Holbrook, Stewart H. *Rivers of America: The Columbia* (New York: Rinehart, 1956). A popular history of the Columbia River basin, with chapters on the Oregon Trail.

Josephy, Alvin M. *The Indian Heritage of America* (New York: Knoft, 1969). A fine general work on the history and culture of the Native Americans.

Lavender, David S. *Westward Vision: Oregon Trail* (New York: McGraw, 1963). A full history of the background and early years of the Oregon Trail.

Merk, Frederick. *History of the Westward Movement* (New York: Knoft, 1978). A full history of the entire American westward movement from sea to sea, including the modern period.

Moody, Ralph. *The Old Trails West* (New York: Crowell, 1963). A brief history of each of the main western trails; includes chapters on the Oregon and California Trails, with excellent maps.

Parkman, Francis. *The Oregon Trail: Sketches of Prairie and Rocky Mountain Life*, 8th ed. rev. (Boston: Little, Brown, 1890). Impressions of life on the Oregon Trail by the noted North American historian.

Schlissel, Lillian. *Women's Diaries of the Westward Journey* (New York: Schocken, 1982). Includes good firsthand accounts of the trip west on the Oregon and California Trails.

Semple, Ellen Churchill. *American History and Its Geographic Conditions* (Boston and New York: Houghton, Mifflin, 1903). A classic work on the influence of geography on patterns of development and settlement in the United States, with excellent maps.

Stewart, George R. *The California Trail* (New York: McGraw Hill, 1962). A useful full treatment of the California Trail, with good maps.

Unruh, John D., Jr. *The Plains Across: The Overland Emigrants and the Trans-Mississippi West, 1840–60* (Urbana, Illinois: University of Illinois Press, 1982; reprint of 1979 edition). A fine history of the overland emigration movement of the period.

Winthur, Oscar Osborn. *The Great Northwest: A History* (New York: Knopf, 1947). A full history of the Pacific Northwest, with chapters on the fur trade and the Oregon Trail.

———. *The Transportation Frontier: Trans-Mississippi West, 1865–1890* (New York: Holt, Rinehart, 1964). A full history of the development of trails, freighting, and railroads in the American West, with excellent maps.

INDEX